CARE
MAGIC

HOW TO GET EMPLOYERS TO WORK FOR YOU

THE NEW REALITIES
OF JOB HUNTING AND CAREER PROGRESSION
– A COMPLETE GUIDE

RYAN STEPHENSON

First published in Great Britain by
ProFile

ProFile
48, Holyrood Road,
Prestwich,
Manchester
M25 1PE

Printed and bound in Great Britain by
Antony Rowe Limited
Chippenham, Wiltshire

Contents

Foreword   1

Introduction   4

1   Surviving Unemployment   9

2   The Concept of Selling   16
    The principals of selling through print   *19*

3   How to Construct a Killer CV   25
    Types of résumé   *28*
    Questionnaire for constructing your CV   *29*
    What never to put on a résumé   *38*

4   The Cover Letter   49

5   Business Realities and the Self-Managed Career Path   59

6   Capitalising On Chaos   71
    A five-point plan for "My Co."   *77*

7   Into the Fray   85

8   Preparing for Interview   95

9   Interview Types   106

10 Clinching the Deal   115
    Great answers to the hardest interview questions   *120*

11 After the Event   132
    Some negotiating tips   *134*

Appendix - action words for CVs   139

Other Reading   146

Foreword

There are those amongst us who have some kind of innate, alien ability to flit from job to job at will, seeking out their most favourable reward wherever they see fit. For the sake of the sanity of us ordinary folk, they are thankfully few and far between. For the majority of us, job hunting is through necessity rather than through choice. Even if, like me, you have a degree or two to your name, don't be fooled into believing this gives you the right to become one of the fortunate few.

You can, however, be forgiven for succumbing to this delusion. Many years ago, when I was graduating for the first time, I thought exactly the same way. With the last exam finally over, I emerged from months of the kind of solitude, darkness and purgatory that would have a Franciscan monk reaching for the travel brochures, into a world of rolling lawns and drifting white clouds suspended in azure skies. The torment was over; a new and prosperous life awaited. Shove a couple of CVs in the post and wait to be snapped up for a fast track career. Doddle!

Oh, poor misguided fool. I went to more 'milk round' interviews than I can remember. I had so many rejection letters, I decorated a whole wall with them. Yes, I know – big psychological blunder. It became a joke. I was making every mistake imaginable. I won't go into what they were now, but as we go through this book together and build a strategy for getting you <u>your</u> job, you can bet your boots that everything you will learn, I didn't do; every trick, I didn't know; every idea, I never had; and every option I didn't consider.

Truth is, getting a job is never easy (at least for the normal people amongst us). Whenever you apply, there are usually certain qualifications stipulated. If you don't satisfy these basic requirements, you won't get invited. If you *do* happen to get an invite, it means you will be competing against people on the same educational and professional level as you. So to pick out one from a hundred similarly qualified candidates, there has to be much more than qualifications that goes into the mix.

Moreover, the higher you go and/or the more qualified you are, the harder it gets: the more committed you're expected to (appear to) be, the more knowledgeable, more communicative, more enthusiastic, more political, more driven, etc., etc., etc. At the one end, you could probably start a job at the supermarket the same afternoon you ask at the job centre. To work in a garage, you may have to do a couple of days proving yourself before they take you on. To become a secretary, may involve a chat with the personnel officer, an interview with the boss and maybe a typing test. To become a marketing manager or software engineer may require, at the very least, an initial interview and an assessment day with half a dozen tests, plus another interview. My own last job took this *and* an extra two interviews.

Anyway, back at University, I eventually, somehow, ended up at British Steel. I probably only got the job because I was talking to two other metallurgists (my degree subject) and so could talk for England about crystal structures and strengthening mechanisms. Yawn.

After 5 years of pretty much stagnation I had got nowhere and indeed had begun to go backwards, having been dropped two grades due to the ritual annual round of redundancies. Sorry…rationalisations.

From then on, it was downhill all the way. So, before I lost my last shred of motivation, I took voluntary redundancy, dusted off my satchel, shook my brain back to life and went back to school. Well, what else was there to do? After completing the MBA, I fell into the same trap – believing I would be snapped up for my qualifications alone. Then again, even the tutors suffered from the same delusions. Another mountain of rejection letters later and reality began to bite. It bit hard and it hurt.

Then, as desperation began to sink in, I made my first progress step. All of a sudden, after a lifetime of going with the flow, of being a good little academic and living inside books, a glimmer of light from the real world broke through the sheened cover. Shock, horror – I had an idea of my own! I asked a couple of the people I had written to why I had been rejected. From their brief replies, I concluded a few important points.

First, I hadn't focused my search closely enough. I'd send the same response to anything which contained key words I recognised – manufacturing, management, productivity, quality, continuous improvement and so on. Second, and partly as a result of this, my CV looked just like all the others – tedious and rather unreadable. Third, I'd tried to include everything in it in the hope that they would pick out the good bits. Lastly, and sometimes most importantly, my cover letter was awful. Now, I chose that word for a reason – that it is a 'nothing' word. It is not specific. Just how awful was it? Why was it awful? Relative to what? What I should have said was "my cover letter was verbose, not concise", or "generic, not specific". It took three minutes to read properly, rather than 20 seconds. It had paragraphs, not points; long sentences, not statements.

After that I started to take note of *exactly* what I was writing and why *every* word was included. What *exactly* should I be saying in response to their ad? Who *specifically* were they looking for? How exactly could I mould my experiences and abilities around their profile?

Just about every letter I sent out from then on differed from the last, as did the CV. Sometimes to alter the layout or appearance and sometimes because of relevance to key points in the job profile. Likewise the cover letter. In the end, I could alter it almost at will, depending upon the precise job title, job profile and to whom I was writing: personnel officer, agency or potential boss. Mind you, it took a couple of years and around 300 applications to get to that stage. By that time, I'd been through more redundancies in a year than most people go through in a lifetime. Three, to be precise. My total is now four, plus a couple of periods as a self-employed consultant.

It's nothing to boast about, of course – going through the mill so many times. OK, bad pun for an ex-steel worker, but it's certainly one of the best qualification for job hunting. I found out, through extensive trial and error cycles, by asking, self-critiquing and continually re-adjusting my approach, just how to get responses and how to be interviewed. I made every mistake in the book – and some not even written. And if you can't learn from your mistakes, you've got no hope.

I certainly wouldn't want you to make the mistakes I did. Obviously, you can't expect to get it perfectly right first time (because there's really no such thing, anyway), but by following the advice and techniques in this book you'll avoid most of them, I assure you.

In this book, you'll find everything you need to know to succeed in your job hunt, without suffering the months of rejection that I had to endure in the early days. As Disraeli said, "The greatest good you can do for another is not to share your riches, but to reveal to him his own."

Introduction

It's a depressing prospect, having to find a job. At least, for many people it is. It's the career equivalent of the disheartening and uncertain vacuum of partner-searching hell. The fruitless sojourns into unknown territory, the social mask, the mind games, the self-doubt, the rejections, the stings.

Just as there are some annoying individuals who breeze through this social quagmire with casual ease, so there are those who have an equally perplexing knack of flitting from job to job whenever it befits them, swinging up the corporate ladder like a hyperactive gibbon.

For most of us, though, the reality is rather more sobering. The need to job hunt can descend upon us from the void in a variety of hideous forms, none of which you would want to invite round for tea and buns.

For months, it can stalk you like a shadow, a dim apparition just discernable in the peripheral vision of your mind's eye, disappearing as soon as you turn your thoughts towards it, your sub-conscious tricking you into believing all is, in fact, well. If you're shrewd, you will see the writing it leaves on the wall and convert your suspicions into planned options. Otherwise, one unsuspecting day, it will leap out and envelop you in its swarthy cloak. You'll be stunned into action too late, leaving you to grapple with the realisation that you should have heeded your feelings of impending doom and planned your escape in advance.

Other times it will descend without warning from the heavens and instantly cloud your vision with the black of night. All colour drains from your world, your plans turn to dust and the castles you have built begin to shake at the foundations.

It has also an ethereal form, which can infect you with a curse. Once so possessed, you are exiled to wander a desolate, twilight steppe as a Career Chameleon, trading your skills in whatever form befits your current situation. You are resigned to trudge an indistinct, winding, rutted and wearisome path to an unlit and continually receding horizon. Still you must tread the path, for you are here by your own decisions, convicted as the only victim of your mistakes, to wander the face of an uncharted land called Your Career.

If you have had to job hunt by necessity rather than by planned choice, you will know what I mean. Any of these debilitating conditions has the potential to beset anyone and the probability of being struck down is increasing all the time. But why is this so?

Well, you could fill a small library with the technicalities: the politics, the economics, the globalisation of trade, the information revolution, demographic trends, and so on. But let's try for a quick summary, anyway.

The previous two recessions saw a sea-change in the industrial map of the nation. Out went heavy industry and with it went the unions, job security and steady promotion. In came services, part-time work and short-term contracts, flexibility and the flat organisational structure. Since then, the information revolution has brought a need for speed to organisations. Quick to act and quick to change.

This in turn has radically altered the definition of a valued employee. For now the means of productivity is no longer the application of labour or analysis by management. It is the knowledge possessed by the workers; the specialisms – those who analyse, compute, devise and assess. This is a range of specialisms no one manager can command. The tools of the trade (computers and information) now move at the speed of utilisation by the worker, rather than the speed set by management analysis. This has shifted the balance of power away from management and freed such employees to apply themselves wherever they may gain most benefit. Management may still determine the requirements of their businesses, but the solutions are no longer derived from throwing labour and capital at them; they come from the application of information and the knowledge to work on that information productively and effectively. So the contractual chains still worn by such enlightened employees are only for show. For it is these "knowledge workers", not the managers, who possess the keys to productivity and, hence, business prosperity.

Working under the guise of commitment to the business, these employees are in fact trading their wares to the highest bidder and are free to move on if circumstances fail to inspire them. While many managers still live in their blinkered world of control, the modern employee is, in reality, operating within management's sphere of influence but outside of their control.

The rapid ebb and flow of competitive position that the speed of information brings, draws into its wake a similarly rapid ebb and flow for labour. Command of appropriate knowledge and flexibility in its application are now the by-words of prosperity.

As a by-product of this mutation of business biology, career services and training companies have multiplied like bacteria, feeding on the insecurity that now pervades the job market. People now move jobs about as often as they move house. Does this point to the need to be continually on the move to find work? Could be! That's how flexible you have to be these days.

Now for employees, there are two distinct sides to this coin of dubious value. On the one hand, it is disaster. With no secure future, you can't even plan your next holiday, let alone your next career move. In a moment, they can pull the rug from beneath years of effort, leaving you all of a sudden stranded.

If you remain, you get piled with more work for the same pay. Do you complain? Not likely! If cancer was the plague of the 20th century, then workplace stress is fast becoming the plague of the 21st. Admittedly it's not such a critical state, but you are about as much use to your life in either condition.

On the flip-side, though, the optimist can see through this dungeon of despair to the chinks of light that tell of fields of opportunity beyond.

And this is what this book focuses on - how to turn the realities of modern working to your own advantage and how to capitalise on this apparent chaos.

We'll look at developing a personal strategy coherent with these realities that will boost your confidence and abilities. We'll see where you can take advantage of these apparent career restrictions and use what others would regard as chains to drag your employer into your line.

And what if they don't want to play? Well, you will have in your possession the most powerful CV you could ever produce. And with it, you will be able to effectively target your ideal job and tackle interviews with confidence and authority. It all adds up to a total package to sustain you through these difficult and trying times. A package based on actual business realities and proven, successful job-hunting techniques. It can be a very unnerving and uncertain time being in the job market. You are often running blind. All you need is a little guidance.

But to make full use of the approach advocated here, we must also understand the technicalities of our labours. Following instruction is not enough, for this does not bring understanding. And it is only through understanding that personal application can be achieved; without it you are simply abiding by a prescription. This is a fundamental error, as will be explained in chapter 5.

Here, too, we will investigate the new realities of the job market place. That successful management no longer depends upon the analysis of work and the application of resources to meet requirements, but in the nurturing of knowledge within employees and in the freedom to apply that knowledge productively. Those organisations that do this will retain their employees; those that cling on to their traditional hierarchical power roles will struggle. This is a point of capital for employees. Understanding this trend will give you the confidence to exercise your freedom in the job market, for which we will build a strategy in the latter chapters of this book.

Inherent to this approach is the realisation that you are a free agent in the job market. And it is not called a "market" for nothing. There is stiff competition, ever-changing demands, new opportunities and fierce sparring for the most valuable quarry on both sides.

So, like it or not, we're talking about selling here. Selling is an awkward concept for some people, I know. But rest easy, we'll ease into it. In any case, the vast majority of work you'll be doing through this book centres on preparation; stuff you can do at home and as you go about your day. So you won't have to worry about trying to sell yourself "cold". Follow the advice in this book and you'll be so rigorously prepared, you won't even know you're doing it. We will be going through a proven battle strategy to help you land a job of your choosing – quickly. And not just this time. The skills and techniques you will learn will give you the confidence and ability to strike out again and again should it come to that.

I make exception here for those currently unemployed. You may not at first be able to secure the job you really want, but have to settle for satisfying your immediate needs. Any port in a storm and all that. You have to be either supremely confident or a little mad to turn down any reasonable offer. You are in a far greater predicament than those looking to move jobs. The urgency is very real. Time is pressing and results are needed. The first chapter, then, is primarily for these people. Some of the points may seem trivial; patronising even. Maybe. But they are all very relevant. The great Charles Darwin was minded to take note of "trifling facts", for though they may seem insignificant, facts they nonetheless are and can still make or break the application of a theory.

Losing your job (and these days it is a very distinct possibility) is always a kick in the face, but it won't seem as daunting, depressing or hopeless as it used to be once you've absorbed and adapted the advice and techniques in this book. *Knowing* that you can tackle the job market will have you back on your feet and fighting for your place while others are still reeling and swirling about in the maelstrom of the search.

So, roll up your sleeves – it's time to get mean. Let battle commence.

1

Surviving Unemployment

Losing your job is a roller-coaster of emotion. And as you go through the long and torrid process of re-establishing yourself, a single thought or event can swing your mood from one extreme to the other. One minute you can see the sky and your hands are in the air, the next your stomach is sinking and you're fighting off fear and despair.

If it comes as a surprise, it can leave you cold. As you walk in the door to be confronted by a couple of solemn faces and dipped (I'd like to think, ashamed) eyes, you know instantly what's coming. A wave of fright sweeps over you from head to toe in a cold sweat. Your legs start to tremble and your mind races, but nothing sticks; thoughts go scudding in and out without so much as a by-your-leave. Meanwhile, on the other side of the table, they spout excuse after excuse for poor performance (never their fault) for no reason except to absolve themselves. What are you suppose to say? "Yes, I agree. In that case I suppose it's only fair that I should go!" Sometimes you just want to cry, either out of desperation, helplessness or pure rage. Usually it's only afterwards you wish you'd had the presence of mind to jam their heads in the coffee pot or feed their briefcase to the shredder (or the other way round!).

There'll be a thousand thoughts jockeying for pole position in your mind. This means, cutting to the chase, the first thing you need to do is get them in order and get an effective plan together. This takes a certain discipline: there are just too many thoughts, all of which need immediate attention.

It's time to STOP: Stop, Think, Observe, Plan.

First, Stop. Stop panicking, stop fretting, stop pouring alcohol down your face, stop blaming others, stop plotting your revenge, stop shouting at your spouse/children/dog. If you've just been laid off, I'm sure you do at least a couple of these things each day.

All of these soak up your time, energy and brain power. You only have a limited amount of "attention space" in your head and it is being swamped by negative and damaging undesirables. You're putting undue stress on yourself and everyone around you – some of whom you are going to rely on for support and understanding in the coming weeks. Job hunting is a hard and stressful occupation as it is, without voluntarily loading yourself down before you begin.

It is excess mental baggage you can well do without. From being secure and comfortable, you've suddenly been dumped in an inhospitable, unforgiving environment. You're out in the cold and you have a mountain to climb. Everybody's well-being depends upon you scaling the summit as quickly as possible. You need two things: a map (your plan of action) and minimum baggage. Then you knuckle down, focus on the summit and look forward to the joy, pride and relief of emerging into the light once more.

You are now free to think clearer, to put your situation in perspective and to set some priority to your thoughts and actions. You should first of all realise that, in the meantime, with at best a reduced income, you *will* have money worries, your children will want for the treats they're used to, you will suffer rejection, you will have to forego your days and nights out and you will feel trapped. And most of all, your pride will take a real hammering. You'll have to decline evenings out, you can't plan holidays, you may have to ditch weekend breaks, planned excursions with friends, the regular Friday night meal out, sell the second car, halt the investment fund contributions. In fact, every time you dip your hand in your pocket, it hurts. You struggle to balance your fear with your pride in maintaining your quality of life.

But that's the path you are on. Millions have trod it before and millions will do so in the future. And many have larger financial commitments than you, less back up, fewer qualifications and a less prosperous business sector to re-apply to. There's only one true and straight path up that mountain and you're going to be on it. However, with planning and discipline, all such things will be pushed to the back of your mind, allowing you to focus on the task in hand – getting back into work. Make the right preparations and have the right focus and you won't get bogged down, get lost in the fog or be diverted from your path.

Once you know what to expect and what you're up against, you will have some perspective on proceedings. It's time to make a checklist of things to do that will allow you to focus on the task in hand. This is your Observation stage. You need to look at:

Family:	They need to know what the situation is. Concealing the truth will only compound your difficulties.
Money:	Bank balances, known expenditures, expected incomes and other buried pots from which you could empty the cash.
Liabilities:	Things you need to ditch to avoid distraction and unnecessary worries and expense, such as those mentioned above.
Job hunt:	How and where you are going to search. You're in luck – you have this book!

The above list is probably the order in which you should work. Before you do anything, your family needs to know the score. They will need to know that the holiday is cancelled until further notice; that Sunday trips are also out; that you may have to work all hours for a while; perhaps you will both need part-time or temporary jobs. They will be affected by the change in family income, the necessary sacrifices, the temporary upheaval in lifestyle and so on.

Your over-riding concern in the above list – the one that falls into all categories one way or another – is money. So let's see what we can do to get an handle on it.

Firstly, you _have_ to know how much you have, where it is going to go over the coming months and where you might be able to get some more. This will tell you how long you have before things get desperate. Then you can develop contingencies well in advance and not be losing sleep over it the night before a key interview. The last thing you need is another major shock right now. Here are some tips for controlling and minimising your expenditure.

1. Get rid of the credit cards.

Cut them up. Yours _and_ your spouses. They're a liability. Do the same with any store cards you might have. You can always re-apply later. Even if you pay your balance in full each month, they encourage you to spend more than you otherwise would. There's nothing like handing over hard cash to make you realise how much things really cost.

With cards, you never really look at the total. Just sign and off you go. Notes you have to count. When you hand over the folding stuff, you can see it, feel it and smell it. Blue ones aren't so bad, but brown ones are difficult to let go of. Purple ones are positively painful to lose and as for red ones, well, I don't think I've seen many of them, so I wouldn't know.

11

Fan out a handful and you literally weep inside as they get stuffed into that bulging cash desk and hidden from your view for the last time.

If you do have overdue balances, you have an extra job to do. You now have to work your ass off to get them paid off. Now. There could be a thousand better things to do with your money than volunteering to give it away through mammoth monthly charges. The three additional steps below can be directed towards this extra goal.

2. Balance your cheque book.

If you haven't got a recent bank statement, ask for one, or go to the machine and order one. Find out where your balances stand. Hopefully you keep your receipts (you can't be sure your statements are correct without them). If so, tick them off against the statement, along with your cheque stubs to see how many have yet to go through. This will give you a balance for a few days hence. If you're sharp, you will have realised already that we are about to build a projected cash flow statement for yourself.

Next, take all your outstanding credit card receipts and add them up. You won't be getting any more (will you?) so that total will be your credit card bill yet to come. Now list all other bills yet to arrive and the dates you are expecting them. Also, make provision for family birthdays and Christmas. When you're satisfied, add up the totals to be paid out each week.

Now comes the good bit. At the bottom of your table, add another row which says "income". Fill in wherever you will be getting some cash in. This may be income-based investments, a redundancy cheque, income support, family credit, your part-time job, a monthly bung off rich Aunt Maude, whatever. List them all separately, as with the out-goings. If you do have investments, you may choose to cash them in. I can't discuss those; you will need to seek proper financial advice.

Add up your total income by week. Subtract your total out-goings from this figure to give your net income by week.

Add one final row for "new balance". This is your balance at the start of the week added to your projected net income for that week. You can now see how your bank balance will change over the weeks. You will therefore have advanced warning of shortages and you will know well in advance when cash will run low. And if it looks like you're not going to get through, you can start doing something about it right now and not panic when the red bills suddenly start spoiling your breakfast.

The finished article should look something like the table at the end of the chapter, which is very similar to the one I have used myself in the past.

In this example, severance pay and one month's notice keep the balance relatively healthy until the new year. There are potential worry spots in November, when the TV license falls due, and at Christmas, but you can see that they are, in fact, covered. If times are really bad, you don't have to pay your licence, though. I'm not saying you should default, you just ship the TV out. You can also suspend your insurance policies as well, even house insurance (as you will be home most of the day). These can save you sums well into three figures every month.

The table shows that basic living expenses are currently affordable even without a part-time job. However, without the severance pay, we are, in fact, insolvent: out-goings are greater than income, so the net weekly income is negative. This allows you to see what sort of income you would need from a part-time or temporary job to stay afloat.

As you have no idea yet how long it will take you to get another job, you should avoid complacency just because the bank balance is currently healthy. It's only human nature to be blasé until predicaments become immediate, so the sooner you realise you *could* get into difficulty, the sooner you will be motivated into action. Now to continue our list.

3. Stop smoking

You'll live longer, too. This is going to really annoy some people. Just ask yourself what comes first: your family's well-being or your own selfish cravings. Your average smoker can literally *burn* £50 to £100 a month on cigs (on 10 to 20 a day). That's £600 to £1,200 per year. If you were offered a pay rise that big, would you turn them down? In effect, it adds up to free food and fuel. If it helps, promise yourself that, when you get another job, you will continue to save this amount, but instead invest it in an ISA for yourself or the kids. Even if you're only a 10-a-day person, in 10 years time, you should have somewhere between 10 and 15 grand coming your way.

Now that's worth a little effort, I'm sure. The easiest way to give up smoking is to stop putting cigarettes in your mouth and lighting them. If you haven't got the guts to do that, there are herbal remedies on the market. Don't scoff. They work. I've seen it.

Chess players know that all pieces are expendable except for the king. If necessary, all other pieces are required to sacrifice themselves for the victory of the king. Your next job is your king.

4. Get a job

Any job. It doesn't matter, it's not for ever. Just don't sign on. Money might be your greatest worry, but as it starts to run out, it can also be your greatest motivator. You should not allow the DSS safety net to be your only support. For it is far from safe. The consumptive predators of despair and sloth lurk there. Once they get a grip of you it can be a real fight to shake them off.

And besides, living off hand-outs is so demeaning. It eats at your pride, your self-worth and your self-esteem. I know we all pay into the pot for just this eventuality, but the value of fending for yourself is far greater than getting those few quid back.

Work for your crust. Get out of bed, get sweaty and get paid. Put up with uneducated, incompetent supervisors, get shouted at for no reason, work horrible hours. In the past I've served drinks in a café, served fruit and veg, scrubbed animal crud from factory trays, cleaned floors, washed pots and emptied out grease traps (the monkey jobs of all monkey jobs), lugged carpets, driven vans, stacked TVs and videos and heavens-knows what else. Every day you do your crappy, insulting little job you get a little angrier. Anger that stokes the fire of your determination to get the hell out of there and back into your own world.

OK, so now you have breathing space. The money is coming in and you know you have enough to last. That's one massive relief, I can tell you. The chaos in your mind subsides and you are free to focus on the main objective of landing another job. This is the process we are now going to start. It'll begin with a look at the principals of selling yourself into the job market and how to succeed in this through a dynamite CV. We'll explore some realities of today's turbulent job market, how to exploit it for maximum gain and how and where to go about patrolling it for your ideal job. Then we'll step through the interview process so that all this hard work comes to fruition.

Example of a weekly cash-flow forecast

Out	Week ending. Sunday																
	03/09	10/09	17/09	24/09	01/10	08/10	15/10	22/10	29/10	05/11	12/11	19/11	26/11	03/12	10/12	17/12	24/12
Starting balance	1850	1335	1315	1245	2665	2030	2010	1820	1800	2730	2175	2155	1885	1865	1300	1280	1210
Gas				60													
Electric										40							
Phone														50			
Water					120												
Mortgage	350			350						350				350			
Pension	100			100						100				100			
ISA			50				50					50				50	
Food	25	25	25	25	25	25	25	25	25	25	25	25	25	25	25	25	25
Extras*	30	30	30	30	30	30	150	30	30	30	30	230	30	30	30	30	180
Total out-going	550	55	105	115	670	55	225	55	55	590	55	305	55	600	55	105	205
In																	
Severance pay				1,500					950								
Family allowance	35	35	35	35	35	35	35	35	35	35	35	35	35	35	35	35	35
Temp. job																	
Total income	35	35	35	1535	35	35	35	35	985	35	35	35	35	35	35	35	35
Net Income	-515	-20	-70	1420	-635	-20	-190	-20	930	-555	-20	-270	-20	-565	-20	-70	-170
New bank bal'ce	1335	1315	1245	2665	2030	2010	1820	1800	2730	2175	2155	1885	1865	1300	1280	1210	1040

* Extras will include petrol, TV license, car tax, MOT, insurance policies, presents and general living.

2

The Concept Of Selling

Selling is a sequential process. No salesperson worth their salt (and who presumably wants to keep their job) will approach a customer with a "Nice isn't it? Do you want to buy it?" pitch. All they're going to get in response to that is "I'm just browsing", "give me a bit of time, please", or just "No, thanks". Customers need to be warmed up. The sales person has to establish a rapport, find out the customer's needs and desires, preferences and biases, narrow the parameters through open questioning, generate the desire in particular options, overcome resistance and then go for the close.

With job hunting, you have to do the bulk of this without the advantage of the face-to-face selling situation. Instead, you have to generate sufficient desire in your prospect purely through the power of your written message; i.e. through your CV.

How? By employing the powerful sales secrets I'm now going to divulge to you. In short, we are going to approach CV writing from an advertising point of view. Let me explain the validity of this approach.

In addition to running the "Career Dynamics" business, I am also a professional copywriter, particularly focusing on direct mail. Direct mail means selling stuff through letters sent directly to prospective customers, as opposed to mail order which is selling through 'space ads' – these are the ones you find in newspapers and magazines. Both are a cheap alternative to a travelling sales person. But the (big) downside is the lack of personal contact. You can't test the ground, get a feel for your prospect or get feedback off them. For this reason, it is widely recognised that direct mail and mail order are the toughest forms of advertising.

With direct mail, you write to people who, when they woke up that morning, had never heard of you before and had absolutely no intention of even considering buying what you are offering. Your sales message has to be so strong and so compelling that, even before they've had their cornflakes, you have persuaded them to open their cheque books.

Mail order is typically no different, with the added constraint that it has to be done in a much smaller space, whilst being surrounded on all sides by other ads vying for attention. To succeed, your advert has to stand out from the barrage of information that is the advert pages. You have to quickly and concisely deliver a clear, benefit-ridden message that draws the reader through your entire advert towards the order form. Hopefully, by the time they get that far, the ad has created enough desire to have them routing for a pen and their credit card.

In both cases, the advert is the sole point of sale. There is no corporate buffer, no monkey-marks for good location and no passing trade. If the advert doesn't sell, it's piles of cash down the pan and a shed-full of stock nobody wants. And that means bankruptcy. The bottom line is, these sales techniques *have* to work. And work they do. The ones you are about to apply to your job hunting campaign have been used by the world's most successful direct mail and mail order entrepreneurs to collectively sell billions of pounds worth of goods the world over.

Of course I'm pushing here to get you to buy into the approach adopted in this section. That's because there are fundamental similarities between this type of advertising and selling yourself through your CV. These forms of adverts sell through the written word alone. They have a matter of seconds to grab the reader's attention and draw them through the rest of the advert.

And it's exactly the same with your CV. If they read but don't buy, well that's just too bad. But if they don't even read, then you've got no chance. Your CV will be competing for the recruiter's time not only against the dozens of others in the pile, but also against the mountain of other work in their diaries. They will be itching for a reason to dismiss you and so get the pile down. If your CV at any time gives them that chance, they will take it. The techniques I am about to unveil will minimise the chances of this happening to you.

Of course, you don't have to use these techniques. But if you don't, you'll either be following the pack, or you'll be in danger of repeating all the mistakes I made as I learnt this stuff.

I get one fleeting chance to sell through my letters and adverts. If there isn't an instant answer to the "WIIFM" question in the reader's mind ("what's in it for me"), it will be ditched. Similarly, your CV is your one and only advert to the world extolling your wares and talents, your career experience and your benefits to prospective employers. When employers scan your CV, you get one brief opportunity to sell your suitability. If you don't get it right, you're binned. In both cases, then, the principals are the same.

Let's not delude ourselves, though. No one can sell to everyone. The world is no-one's oyster. Any product can only be sold to a limited section of the population. To sell successfully through the mail, you have to know and understand the kind of person who represents that section. Then you must write in a manner that will appeal to them and offer them benefits that promise to improve their life in some way.

Again, it's exactly the same with your CV. Firstly, it has to be tailored specifically towards the kind of job that you want. Then you have to demonstrate in only a few lines that you have the capability of improving their business in some way.

But even then, it won't succeed every time. Why not? Well, lots of reasons. Basically, it boils down to the fact that employers are only people. They're not gods. And businesses go bust every day. If these people are successful in understanding and satisfying a market demand, they will make money and survive. If they don't, they won't. These same bosses usually have a direct hand in recruiting and in making choices on who is best for them. When a business flags, the people in it have made mistakes. Not choosing the right people will almost certainly be one of those mistakes.

So if you get rejected, it may not be your fault. Their recruitment process may be ill-conceived, they may have less than a solid idea of who best fits the bill or perhaps their preferred profile is flawed in the first place. Perhaps they just don't know what they're doing. But even if it is, don't take it personally. It may take you a few goes to fine-tune your approach. Give some extra thought to the ideas in this book and pass a critical eye over your work.

And remember, your task here is doubly difficult, because you're dealing with people. Imperfect, moody, possibly uneducated, biased, stuck-in-their-ways, maybe bored, maybe tired, self-interested, egotistical human beings. You can't account for those variables in your equations.

Because of this inherent human element, there are no hard and fast rules to this game. But it does have a distinct nature to which you can adapt. Knowing how the game is played will allow you to swing the odds in your favour. And I'll be giving you all the insights you need to do this.

I hope that just about covers it and that you can begin to appreciate the relevance of this approach. I want to emphasise that these techniques have been proven to work in selling through print, year in, year out. And your CV is itself nothing more than a sales message in print. We will now begin looking at the principals of constructing this message.

The Principals Of Selling Through Print

Successful marketing is critical to a successful business. It's a fundamental fact. You can have the best product in the world, but if you don't market it right, it will fail. In job hunting, your CV is your advert.

First of all, think for a moment what happens when you look through the advert pages of a newspaper. Do you spend your valuable time reading meticulously through each advert? No, you 'skim'. Your eyes settle on the one that stands out. It is bold and concise and immediately spells out the benefits to you, the customer, of having this product. This is just one of the direct similarities between a good CV and good advert copy. Other elements of a successful advert relevant to producing a good CV are:

1. The headline. It should:

- Grab the reader's eye; get attention.
- Select the audience; it appeals to the kind of people who would be interested in the product.
- Summarise the whole offer; there is a full sales message.
- Speak directly to you, the buyer.
- Entice the reader to continue reading.

By analogy, your headline will be your cover letter and your job objective. They will be targeted specifically towards the job you are applying for and give a full and solid summary of your principal qualifications and abilities. This will imply to the reader that perusing the detail in your CV will be time well spent.

2. The body copy (the main text).
Compelling, interesting body text has the following properties:

- It supports and expands on the headline.
- It is full of benefits, substantiated by features. This is important; we'll cover it later in some detail.
- It makes the sale in as many words as is necessary, but not one more. "Concise, key and relevant" are three critical words here.
- The features and benefits list is the source of the copy.
- It uses short sentences and simple words.
- It avoids wordy phrases (don't use 4 words where 2 will do):
  e.g. A wide variety of = A range of;
      Expert in the field of = Expert at;
      Have several years' experience in = 5 years in/as.
- It avoids duplicate words:
  e.g. 'Variety of different' is repetition; use either 'variety' or 'different';
      Many varied fields / duties = many fields / duties.
- The benefits are prioritised and only the most important ones are included.
- Overstate the product by all means, but it must be honest.
- It uses 'benefit-generator' words. These convert features into benefits (e.g. ensure, enhance, maximise). A full list of benefit-generator words can be found in the appendix.
- It is specific; uses numbers and facts:
  e.g. A wide range of = 25 (or whatever number);
      Experience in = 5 years in.
- It uses white space to good effect; dense copy is a formidable proposition.

This is all relatively self-explanatory. I hope with just that list you are beginning to see where this is going. As you progress through the following sections and begin constructing your own CV, you will see each of these points emerging.

3. Features and Benefits

This is a vital concept, supposedly known by many but applied by few. Distinguishing between features and benefits is in the top 3 skills required to create compelling copy (along with understanding why and how people buy and how to construct killer headlines). It is equally important in your CV.

For example, a two-inch long sliver of wood with a red phosphorous tip is a description of a match, but they are sold as cheap, convenient, portable fire, useable without heat. A fork is a cheap, 3-pronged piece of 18% chrome-6% nickel steel with a curved handle, but it is bought as a re-useable, hygienic means of spiking food, which is long-lasting, easy-to-clean, stain-resistant and visually appealing.

In these simple examples, the former descriptions are the features; the latter lists are the benefits. It is the benefits that satisfy the needs. These are the pieces of information that spell out the enhancements you will bring to the organisation you apply to and so are the ones you should be emphasising in your CV. Benefits support your job objective. They prove that, by hiring you, the employer will be better endowed than it was before. They will, for example, be better at selling, more efficient, better prepared, better controlled, more systemised, more creative, more profitable, etc.

The way to think about benefits is to ask yourself "How will this make life better for my prospect?" This is a principal reason why I mentioned earlier that it is important to understand who your prospect is. Here it will be prospective employers, targeted through your job objective. The more benefits you can come up with, the greater will be the support for your potential to fulfil your job objective and so the stronger will be your claim to be the right person for the job itself.

Here's a useful exercise you can try. I wrote the notes for this book in biro. The features and benefits of a biro are listed in the following table.

Try this yourself on any old object. It's a good exercise to get you to look deep into your work history, to identify how you can be of benefit to employers.

When you come to write down your work history, it will be easier to be autobiographical at first. These are your features; the tasks you have done at previous companies. For each feature, you should be able to come up with related benefits for the employer, which will then be listed in your principal abilities (or similarly named) section. The benefits serve to generate desire in the employer's mind; to create the feeling that you can be of value to them. The features provide the rationale for the employer; the proof of this emotional decision; the justification for calling you in.

The features and benefits of a biro.

Feature:	Benefit:
6" long	It is well-balanced in the hand and gives long life.
$^1/_3$" diameter	Easy and comfortable to hold.
Clear, tough polycarbonate outer	Lightweight, robust, long-lasting. Can see how much ink is in the cartridge.
Transparent plastic inner	Lightweight. Can see how much ink is left in the cartridge.
Inner is removable	Can easily and cheaply replace ink cartridge to extend the life of the pen and keep costs to a minimum.
Removable plastic blue cap	Covers the tip to prevent marking. Shows the colour of the ink in the pen at a glance and is easy to spot if dropped.
Cap inner has equal diameter to barrel	Cap can be re-fitted to top of pen for convenience and to prevent it being mis-placed.
Cap has narrow, flexible extension	Allows pen to be clipped to pocket or clothing for convenience and safe keeping.
Cap has a hole in the top	For safety, this allows air passage if accidentally swallowed.
Secure blue plastic top plug	Prevents ink leakage and, for safety, cannot be removed.
Narrow ball tip	For smooth, accurate, easy-to-read writing.
Blue ink	Clear, distinctive and permanent.

A few examples to illustrate:

Feature	Benefits
5 years experience in steel melting *(now applying to be a lab. manager).*	Fully conversant in applied steel metallurgy. Excellent man-manager. Highly knowledgeable of applied quality control to ISO9000, Ford Q1 and aerospace standards. Experienced in auditing procedures. Intimate knowledge of production processes.
3 years using MRPII *(now applying for logistics manager).*	Skilled in the organisation and analysis of complex logistics. Skilled in cost control and reduction. Fully conversant with operational and supply channels.
5 years in care homes, progressing to ward sister *(now moving locations).*	Renowned for forbearance with patients. Experienced and congenial communicator with colleagues and public. Proven organisational ability.
5 years as Inland Revenue clerk *(now applying to be tax accountant).*	Fully skilled in all aspects of processing public tax returns. Highly experienced in communicating information clearly and accurately. Demonstrated diplomacy when dealing with clients.
3 years as human resources officer *(now moving into health and safety).*	Excellent practical knowledge of business legislation. Experienced in industrial relations. Skilful negotiator. Experienced in developing and implementing employee training programmes.

In the above examples, I deliberately chose a few job-switchers to illustrate the need to extract only those aspects of your career to date which are pertinent to the new job. It is often more difficult for job switchers to determine these points. The section on skills identification on page 78 will help.

In the first example, the first four points are all important to being a lab. manager. The last one would be top of the list if applying to be a steel-maker, but now it is relegated to a useful extra, enabling detailed understanding of problems encountered on the shop-floor. For the ward sister, I have listed (with apologies to real nurses) the softer* qualities as being most important, as the comfort of and compassion towards the patients will be a primary concern.

Now we are going to apply these principals to your own CV.

---

* In a nutshell, the 'hard' approach is defined, instructional, written, specified; the 'soft' approach is personal, inter-personal, cognitive, non-quantifiable.

3

How To Construct A Killer CV

This is the most critical part of the whole job-hunting process. This is the foundation for your entire job hunt, as you will soon discover. Your CV will, first and foremost, be your national advertising campaign. You have only one product – you – and it needs to be sold quickly to the highest bidder from perhaps only a handful of interested buyers. You therefore need to do a quite excellent job of selling it. This means you need to be intimately familiar with the features and benefits of the product and be consummately professional in its presentation. To do this will require great preparation. Follow the instructions in this section and the process of producing your CV will prepare you for your job hunt and interviews in more ways than you thought possible. Proper Planning Prevents Poor Performance.

By making CV writing the first stage in your job-hunting process, as we will do now, your chances of rapid success will be greatly increased. Rather than scanning the job pages for key words you recognise and then throwing your life story at them, you should be creating a CV targeted at your chosen job objective and then approach prospective organisations with this 'proof of capability'. With this approach, you will have already done much of the hard work behind your interview preparation.

However, we are jumping the gun a little here, although we can already draw one fundamental conclusion: that it is wholly insufficient to simply list your personal history and hope they will find something of interest in there. You need to identify key qualities that are most appealing to prospective employers and then present them in a fashion that will have them reaching for their phones. Let's draw a quick analogy.

There are 100 VCRs in an electrical store. You've never seen or studied them before and you don't know what they do. You've got a full afternoon (4 hrs) to select one. Could you do it? Probably. But how? Not by careful study and consideration of all the individual machine specifications and comparing them against each other. Mind-numbing tedium. Instead, after studying the first few, you realise that there are certain similarities between them – features you do like and features you don't. So you then start to skip along the lines looking for your preferred features, ignoring the rest. The further you go, the narrower your search parameters get. Eventually your selection is down to a select few. Only then do you consider the finer points of your finalists, to come to a calculated decision.

With actual CV filtering, we are probably being a bit generous here. A few (interrupted) half hours over the course of a week is more like it. A frustrating prospect for anyone. The sooner it's over with, the better! So your CV needs to be sharp and attention-grabbing. It needs to quickly and clearly reveal to your reader your undoubted suitability. That's why the benefits you present have to be concise, key and relevant.

Another thing: do you think your choice of VCR would be a "definitely, no question about it, this is the best" kind of decision? Or would it be a bit of a mental toss-up between two or three favourites? Unless there's one for £200 that telepathically knows which programmes you want to record and saves you the bother of remembering, it's most likely to be the latter. A bit of gut feeling and personal preference creeps in, along with boredom and the desire to get on to something a bit more productive.

Again, candidate selection is no different. So don't be too disheartened if you're not always selected. You can't please everyone.

So let's begin with the basics and examine the purpose of a CV.

The Purpose Of Your CV

The principal objective of your CV is to get you into interview. Once you're there, you can give them as much detail as they want. But for now, you just have to make sure you get there.

So a résumé is not an autobiography. You should not expect the employer to sift through your entire career and pick out the good bits; you should do that for them. Put yourself in their seat. Another morning. It's been a typically torrid half hour through the rush hour. What you need is ten minutes peace and the world's strongest coffee – the kind that would get Rip van Winkle kicking like a mule. Instead, there are a hundred unopened envelopes, each containing a CV pleading for your attention. Ideally, you want to shuffle through the unopened envelopes and telepathically pick out the best one. Unfortunately, you're resigned to spending the whole day reading them all – on top of the two-hour management meeting, the employee hearing to attend, the training programme to review and yesterday's figures to analyse. And it's only half past eight in the morning!

The first task, therefore, is to sift out as many of the dopes as possible: the no-hopers, the under-qualified, the dreary, the inexperienced and so on. If you're not immediately struck by the qualities you're looking for, you haven't got the time or the will to dig into two or three pages of text and translate indistinct phrases into concrete benefits. Now where's that bin…?

Now imagine getting one that *is* concise, that *does* display clear achievements, facts, figures and relevant examples that reflect the job profile. Excellent. One for the 'Yes' pile. Now you have an idea of what you're after; there's a standard to work against. Now the rest have to be as good as, or better than, this one. The filtering gets quicker.

This kind of process goes on every day in all kinds of firms across the land. If your CV isn't up to scratch, it is so easy to get rejected, even when you think you're made for the job. The preparation you are about to do for your CV will make sure it doesn't get absently skimmed and rejected, but instead winds up on top of the stack.

The second role of your CV is as valuable preparation for interview. By picking out relevant, concrete examples, you are indirectly preparing yourself for guaranteed interview questions. Your answers will be prepared and focused. You will appear confident, knowledgeable and professional.

Thirdly, it is your networking tool. It will be precise enough for anyone to pick it up and realise straight away if you will be of value to them. You won't have to be there in person to put your case. It can be working quietly in the background for you.

Before we begin to actually construct your CV, it would be advantageous if we covered the types of CV format you can use. Hopefully, you will instinctively know from your career so far which one is most suitable for you from the following descriptions.

Types of Résumé

1. Chronological
This is the most common type. It lists your jobs in reverse chronological order. Use this format if:

- You have progressed through the ranks;
- You have had a steady progression through a number of companies;
- You have been and intend to stay in the same career;
- Your list of work experience is stronger and more definitive of your abilities than a list of specific achievements.

If it is difficult for you to come up with concrete figures to highlight your achievements to date, then a history of progressively increasing responsibility will help compensate for that.

2. Functional
If the opposite of the above is true for you, use this format; i.e.

- You have little skill or experience yet to speak of;
- You haven't progressed in a logical manner;
- Your current job is less impressive than previous one(s);
- You are switching careers;
- Your list of accomplishments says more about your abilities than your list of past positions.

The functional format focuses on principal skills, rather than job titles.

Since you always need to put dates on your CV, if there are gaps in your work history, consider also using this format. In a chronological format, the date gaps would clearly show and distract the reader from your impressive work history. The functional format relegates the dates list to the second half of the CV. To bias the reader in your favour before any faults are uncovered, your list of achievements and abilities comes first. If they do then discover a gap or two, they will find it difficult to go back on their first, positive, feeling of suitability.

3. Combined

If you lie somewhere between these two, you can use this format. This is suitable for people who have progressed, but maybe not in a logical fashion or always in the same field, but have progressed nonetheless. Here you can list your accomplishments and achievements in descending chronological order (hence the name).

This format is particularly suitable for specialists. Career receptionists, administrators, teachers, scientists, journalists, nurses, solicitors and other such professions and even CEOs will fit this format well. People in these professions will often have accumulated specialist capabilities over the years. Putting these in reverse chronological order shows how their specialism has developed.

In whatever format you create your CV, it will all centre around a specific job objective, which we will now cover. The following pages contain an exercise in the form of a questionnaire. This will help you bring to the surface all the most relevant information about your career and focus it towards this job objective. Remember, this part is vital; take your time and make it good.

Questionnaire For Constructing Your CV

Each of the following 10 questions has accompanying guidance notes to ensure your answers really hit the mark. The information you select in response to these questions is absolutely crucial in producing a winning résumé. The questions have been meticulously prepared to generate your personal winning message. Read the guidance notes carefully to get the most from each. Spend as much time as is necessary answering them. Ask others for their opinion if you like. When you're finished, put it to one side for a day or two, then re-read it. You'll have a fresh perspective on what you have written. This will be your national advert; it's worth every effort.

Remember, this is your national advert. The format you choose will determine whether you highlight your experience, your achievements or your specialism. This, together with your stated job objective, will be reflected in your cover letter and will form your CV headline. The best advert copywriters often spend longer agonising over their headlines than they do over the rest of the advert. No matter how well qualified or eminently capable of doing the job you really are, if it fails in its primary aim of getting the reader's attention and sparking their interest, then all your work will have been in vain.

Q 1 - What specific position are you seeking?

This is *the* most important piece of basic information. The entire résumé will be constructed around this. This is your job objective, pure and simple. It is essentially the job title you seek. So spell out the exact position you are seeking. Make sure it is as specific as possible.

The objective not only tells the employer that you are positive about and focused on the position you seek, but it also gives the reader an immediate reminder of their frame of reference. As all the evidence in your CV will be in support of this objective, when they come to read your career highlights, it will create a clear, complete image of you and your suitability.

If you are considering switching careers, though, a little thought may be required. There could be a number of options to which you could apply your skills. You have two choices. You can either bite the bullet and choose which one appeals to you most or you can construct one CV for each of your options. Because your objective statement will be different for each, the key qualifications and experience details you will pick out later, in support of your objective, will also be different.

Unless you are convinced you are making the right move, my advice is this. Research each of your options. Thoroughly. Delve into the type of businesses you are looking at. What are the relative salary expectations? Is that sector growing, in stagnation or decline? Your local TEC should be able to give you some research detail on this. So can Mintel reports. Mintel is the trade name for the organisation regarded as the bees knees of mainstream market intelligence (m-intel...geddit!). They produce reports covering all kinds of business sectors from brewing to banking, Internet to insurance, health foods to holiday parks. Their reports are not cheap (about £400 each, I believe), so they will generally only be found in principal libraries, rather than your local OAP drop-in centre. The reports are either in bound volumes or on CD-ROM.

While you're in the library, scan the other CD-ROMs for business profiles and newspaper reports on typical businesses in each sector. And, of course, check out the job advert pages for the kind of job profiles you can expect.

And lastly, what is your gut feeling about your options? Which one inspires you? From all the facts you have uncovered, which one offers the greatest personal benefits? Career changers make big decisions. You should get as much information as possible before committing yourself. Don't find out the hard way.

Getting back to your job objective, avoid general words and phrases such as 'challenging position', 'forward looking company', 'communication skills', 'next step', etc. They don't tell the reader *specifically* what you are looking for. And if you don't know where you want to be, how are they going to know if you'll fit? Unfortunately, these are the kind of phrases you often see in job adverts, so it's no wonder candidates copy them. This can, ironically, work to your advantage, as the sudden appearance of a focused CV can act as a wake-up call to the employer that here is someone who knows how to cut to the chase.

Three tips to help you write your objective:

1. Make it as concise as possible.
2. Specify the position you seek.
3. Specify the company you are aiming at.

A few examples:
- A European sales co-ordinator in a blue chip company.
- A research biologist for a small biotech company.
- A branch managerial position in a major UK bank.
- A personal assistant to a director of a FTSE250 company.
- A human resources assistant in a manufacturing SME[*].
- A recruitment consultant to the education sector.
- A college lecturer and researcher in the field of archaeology.
- A position as a tax trainee in a large accountancy firm.
- A key management position in MIS[*] to add to the bottom line growth of a corporation.
- Contract MS Access development.
- Men's apparel buyer for a major department store.
- Data entry clerk within a FTSE250 company.
- A position as senior corporate executive, preferably chief executive officer, of an internationally oriented, publicly traded corporation.

---

* SME = small to medium enterprise.
MIS = management information systems.

Once you're happy with your job objective, it's time to move on. Bear in mind that you are not writing your autobiography. You are picking out the most relevant pieces of your career history that will tell a prospective employer that you are the right person for the job. You are aiming to isolate the key qualifications and abilities that immediately tell the employer you can be of real benefit to them.

Q 2 - List the specific jobs you have held, with dates. For each, list the specific tasks you did. Do these tasks support the position you are applying for?

This is where you begin to get into the body of the CV. You first of all want to list, in reverse chronological order, the separate positions you have held. In each, isolate those key tasks you did, the ones that made the most benefit and the most impact; the ones that defined your role and your success in it.

Note that Question 4 deals with the precise figures of your achievements. For now, you want to be isolating, from all the tasks you performed in the jobs you have listed, those which demonstrate your ability to do the job you are applying for. For example, managers may write their own production reports, but how you devised the performance indicators is more important. If you are a technician, being able to compile quality reports when the quality guy is absent shows your diversity, but you're not applying to be a quality co-ordinator, you want to be a technician – so emphasise your technical abilities. If you used to be a production planner and now you want to be a desktop engineer, extract only those qualities of a planner that are relevant to your new position, say PC skills and problem analysis.

Refer to the example CVs at the end of this section if you wish.

It should now be becoming clear whether your experience and job progression is more significant than your accomplishments. If the former is the case, you will most likely want a chronological format; if the latter is more prevalent, you should consider a functional format. Refer back to the notes on pages 27 and 28 to make sure you have got the right one.

Q 3 - What words best describe the way you performed these tasks?

Spend a little time here and then come back to it later. In the appendix, you will find a comprehensive list of 1,000 "action" words. These are the benefit-generator words which will transform your duties into accomplishments, add strength to your descriptions and bring assertiveness to your testimony. When describing your tasks and achievements, aim to start each of your sentences with one of these words. You don't have to scan them all. They will be cross-referenced in any thesaurus, including the one on your PC. Type in, or look up, a reasonably suitable word, then pick from your options.

One word of advice in selecting the appropriate word: don't undersell yourself. Words can be viewed in many different lights and interpreted in many different shades of meaning. So you'll never be mis-leading your reader, you are simply being positive about your abilities.

Here are some examples of weaker and stronger words:

Weaker	Stronger
Supervised	Managed
Administered	Directed
Dealt with	Negotiated with
Changed	Transformed
Improved	Enhanced, maximised
Informed	Advised
Helped	Assisted, aided, coached
Set up	Created, initiated
Started	Established
Experienced	Expert, skilled

You get the idea.

Q 4 - For each position listed, what definitive contributions or improvements did you make?

Here you want specific numbers or percentages. This data may take a little digging for. You could perhaps analyse how your workload has changed (for the better) while you have been doing that job, or how your contribution to the business has increased or been noted: e.g. tighter delivery schedules, buying discounts, greater repeat business, faster order processing, higher marketing response, reduced tax liability, reduced entry mistakes, improved costing accuracy, bottom-line savings, reduced head-count, increased productivity, etc.

Ideally, you want actual, concrete figures:
- 10% productivity improvement.
- 5% reduction in man-power.
- 15% cost savings.
- Reduced set-up times by 17%.
- Increased sales by £250,000.
- Reduced wastage by £50k p.a.
- Order processing time decreased by 12%.
- Customer returns reduced by 7%.

Where possible, use "funny money". This is a sales term for putting figures in their best light. Charities do it when they ask you to contribute 50p a day. Really, that's almost £200 a year, but who's going to hand over two hundred quid? Insurance companies try the same trick when they say you can have peace of mind for the price of your daily paper. No one really notices their newspaper costs, but they'd take note of £250 a year. Similarly, a reduction in wastage of 0.5% sounds piffling, but it can mean thousands of pounds over a year. Conversely, increasing output by 1,000 widgets per week might only be a fraction of a percentage, but it looks impressive and you can also equate it to a pure profit figure if they ask.

Whatever you say, though, please, please, please... don't get creative; keep the figures real! By the way, when you start a new job, it would be worthwhile taking notes on your performance measures. Then, when you leave, you'll have some hard evidence to put on your CV.

Q 5 - What is your highest academic qualification? Include academic awards or honours.

e.g. A-level physics, applied mathematics, economics. The first time your CV is read, the employer will spend very little time on it. Only later will they ask questions. You can take advantage of this by giving just your highest qualification. If you have a string of A-grades, list them, otherwise leave the grades out. Employers are always looking for a reason to dismiss you. Putting lower grades next to your qualifications enables them to do just that. So leave them off. If your degree is with Honours, include that, too.

For those who got that far, if your thesis or dissertation is directly relevant to the position you seek, include it, otherwise leave it out; the fact that you have a doctoral will impress them enough.

Q 6 - What special skills can you offer to the position you are seeking?

These are particular, tangible skills that you could be tested on if necessary. These will probably be listed separately on your CV as "key abilities" or "principal skills". The more you can list which apply directly to your job objective, the better you will look. Give levels of proficiency in each. In specific cases, you could include such things as accountancy packages, payroll software, MRP I & II, relational databases, HTML, CAD version, lab. analysis techniques and equipment, DTP, SPC applications, statistical analysis or programming languages. You could also include proficiency in certain computer packages, experience with the Internet, foreign language competencies. Clearly for higher managerial positions, your bottom line results will be of primary concern – knowledge of any of the above is a bonus.

Q 7 - Do you belong to any professional associations? Have you held any positions in these groups?

For recent graduates, this may not apply. Instead, include such things as business clubs, social societies, community work, the TA, charity work, etc. Affiliations to professional bodies are often taken as dedication to your field. Some of these associations are actually useful, some aren't. Sometimes you have to take exams to progress through their levels; sometimes it is more a question of time as a member and your position in the company. Some people subscribe just so they can add it to their CV.

Q 8 - Have you ever been published? Where?

This will not apply to everyone. Likely candidates are scientists, graduates, management specialists and, naturally, journalists, writers, researchers and the like.

Q 9 - Why are you the very best candidate for this position?

This is essentially your USP (unique selling proposition). This is where you emphasise your key qualities and achievements. The qualities you pick here will also go on your cover letter. On page 19, we emphasised how the headline must fulfil four essential functions, with the sole aim of encouraging the reader to progress further into your CV.

Here, then, you pick out the essence of your career to date, insofar as it relates to your job objective, and put it as the first line in your "key abilities" or "key qualifications" section. For example:

- 10 years progressing to managing one of the largest city-centre branches of a major UK bank.
- 7 years as a nurse from ward sister to intensive care supervisor.
- 6 years progressing to secretary for site manager.
- 3 years developing web-sites for minimum £10m turnover clients.
- Fluent in German, allowing me to do business internationally for over 7 years.
- 4 years experience managing world class manufacturing environments.

You'll notice how the first three in the above list are more for the chronological format, being derived from work histories with a clear, logical progression or a definite sequence of development. The latter three are more functional. Progression is not mentioned. In its place is a key skill or quality relevant to the position.

If you read back through your answers so far, you should find the one thing that stands out, that you can boast about the most, that, when put on paper next to other CVs, will be your "fingerprint" and says "this is me; this is what makes me stand out". Ideally, it should get to the core of your stated job objective. That way, your USP will be a wake-up slap in the face to recruiters. Persuasive stuff!

Q 10 - Why should <u>you</u> be hired over all the other applicants?
Plays on the same theme as question 9, but with the subtle difference in that it emphasises how you will contribute to the success of the prospective company. Q 9 is your principal feature; here you give your major benefits. Again, this will go on your cover letter. Continuing from the above examples, they may read:

Expert in all aspects of major retail banking.
Increased profits by up to 12% per year.

Highly experienced in a multitude of patient care scenarios.
Skilled in operation of sophisticated patient monitoring equipment.

Fully accustomed with all manner of modern communication and office technology.
Meticulously organised, efficient and proactive.

Average increase in client business through web-sites of 45%.
Excellent referral conversion rate of 1 in 3.
Initiated design protocol library.

Uniquely experienced in all aspects of European supply, marketing, after-sales and customer relations.

Intimately familiar with analysis, development, implementation and control of appropriate production methods and best practice.

And finally...

You need to include a minimum of two references you would like to use. There is no reason why an employer should need references before you are considered for the job. So these will not go on your CV, but will be provided on a separate sheet, which you take with you to interview. Two is the standard number; three is more rare; special occasions may require four. For each reference, include: name, job title, company name, company address and their contact phone number. All you need put at the bottom of your CV is "References: Available on request."

Piecing it Together

Congratulations, the hard work is now done. You have not only done the framework for your CV, but you have also done a fair chunk of your interview preparation. What you have written you *will* be interrogated on; but you have already thought long and hard about these answers and know that they are your best points. Because of this, come interview day, your interviewers will be focusing on your strengths, and you will have ready answers.

Now comes the time to piece it all together. To save long-winded explanations, a few example CVs are given at the end of this chapter, where you can see how the finished article will look once the above process has been applied. There are 2 examples of each of the 3 generic types of CV: chronological, functional and combined. You will already know which format you will be using, what your key abilities are, your principal accomplishments and your relevant work experiences. Now you need to prioritise them and group them under the correct headings.

Try not to take too much notice of the detail in the supplied examples, as they are all invention. It is the format we are interested in, how the key points are presented which support the job objective, the language and the benefit-generators that are used.

Each example is necessarily rather truncated. In yours, you will need to include as many features and benefits from your positions as are pertinent to your job objective. That will mean omitting points that you may feel are significant, but which actually bear little or no relevance to your job objective. You may also choose to keep out lesser, relevant points for the benefit of conciseness. Re-read the 'body copy' notes on page 20 for guidance.

What Never To Put On A Résumé

Your résumé is your professional business profile. It concisely highlights the principal reasons why you are the best person for the job. You want to avoid any distractions from that. Just because something is specified in the advert, doesn't mean to say you have to give it. Employers generally know about as much about what makes a good CV as your average job hunter. What's more, employers are only human (at best!); discrimination does occur, however slight. So does personal favouritism and bias. To avoid presenting any opportunity to exercise these 'qualities', you should omit the following six things from your CV. This will also keep it to the bare essentials and avoid wasting valuable space and the even more valuable time of your reader.

1. Salary expectations. This is just an indirect way of discerning who may be under-qualified or inexperienced and so weeding them out, along with anyone who might ask for too much. You can assume here that the employer wants a highly qualified person for a low price and will discount anyone who ups the ante. Salaries are for post-interview negotiation. If salary is one of the more important stipulations of the employer, it is likely to be a weak organisation. Good ones will pay handsomely for the right person – one who can create returns and benefits that far exceed remuneration.

2. Personal details. Determining your suitability on age is generally discriminatory, so don't give them the opportunity to do so. Your marital status is also irrelevant, except in Japanese car plants. The Japanese prefer a stable family background – they believe it avoids distractions and enhances commitment. The UK, however, is a very different culture. If and how they get away with this policy here, I couldn't say. Nor should your health be a factor, within reason. If you have some kind of recurring illness that continues to keep you away for 50% of the time, it will arise through the references anyway. The only thing you include is your contact details.

3. Your photograph…unless you want to be a model or an air hostess or something with similar close public contact, where personal presentation is very important. Despite what is moral and just, books *are* judged by their cover. You *will* be pigeon-holed by your looks. Anyway, for a start it'll need to be a good photograph. This means a professional photographer and not one of those high-street tardis booths that can make even Ghandi look like America's Most Wanted. Secondly, you may look like the person their spouse ran off, the loony next door who plays music at all hours, one of their parents, the school bully, anything. They may not like black hair, fat people, military-style haircuts, or hints of ethnic descent. A pretty sick list of neuroses, you will agree, but these people exist. If they didn't, there would be no discriminatory laws or equal rights laws and much less need for industrial tribunals. Just because they wear a suit and get paid more than you, doesn't for one minute mean they are fine, upstanding, morally-sound citizens.

4. Your ideal job. You don't go into a travel agent and tell them what your ideal holiday would be; you look for something reasonable that you can afford. What you stipulate is a function of your past experiences and preferences within the constraints of time and money. Then you see if they have a suitable match. Unless you're fortunate enough to be in the type of job that you just l-e-r-r-rve doing, then your ideal job statement is going to be a lie. You might be a computer engineer, but your ideal job would be a fighter pilot (it's not your fault you wear spectacles). There's no saying that a corporate chairman wouldn't rather be a classic car restorer. Any ideal job you could reasonably state is going to be constrained by your experiences, qualifications and salary level. In other words, it will be your job

objective. Ideal job statements are therefore, at best, mis-guided; more likely untrue and, in any case, wholly irrelevant. Leave it off.

5. Gimmicks. Use white paper, water-marked, if possible, and a high 'gsm' (grams per square metre). This is how papers are graded. Standard photocopier paper is 80 gsm. Good, professional writing paper is called 100gsm Vellum bond. Don't use coloured paper, pretty borders, graphics, fancy fonts or type faces or tea-bags. This is true - somebody once 'joked' that the reader would be so stunned by his qualifications, he stapled a tea-bag to the bottom of his CV to revive his reader afterwards! Not! It's a sales gimmick occasionally employed to useful effect, but not here.

6. References. These are only necessary once you have an offer. There's no reason why employers should want them now. Besides, it helps to condense your CV – psychologically important when getting some-one to read it thoroughly. So have these on a separate sheet of paper to take with you to interview.

Final Notes

The precise layout of the CV (the bolds, underlines, font sizes, line spacings, justifications, etc.) is up to you. Everybody's will look different. Just ensure it is clear, appealing to the eye, that your major points spring right out and that you haven't included irrelevant details. When you're done, leave it for a day or two, then go back to it and ask yourself the following questions:

- Does it look visually appealing at first glance, or a formidable block of text?
- Is my job objective clear, concise and accurate? Can I rephrase it to make it shorter?
- Have I chosen the correct format? If your work experience list is longer than your accomplishments and abilities list, but is relegated to the bottom half of the CV, you should switch formats. If, at first glance, there are glaring gaps in your career dates, you should switch formats.
- Are my major achievements and principal abilities top of those respective lists?

- Have I chosen the strongest action words?
- Have I included clear, concrete figures where possible?
- What is my USP? Is it obvious? Is it at the top of my CV?
- Have I included as many benefits as possible?

Clearly, you can carry on like this till Doomsday. So here's another crucial rule of selling: "Sell first, ask questions later." In other words, as long as you have a saleable product, which is well presented, get it (your CV) into the marketplace. You will make greater improvements with a little objective feedback than you would by staring subjectively at it for another week.

And let's face it, with the information and secrets you have just applied and what you are still yet to learn in subsequent chapters, you will knock the socks off 99% of the opposition straight away. So go to it.

Examples of CVs

The following are introductory notes to the example CVs that appear on the following pages.

Chronological CV #1

Previously, I mentioned that there are no hard and fast rules to this game. And this is just such an example. From what has been said before, you might expect a scientist to use a combined résumé and that is certainly one option here. Instead, there are some impressive statistics to be highlighted, so I presented these in the 'key abilities'. Other key aspects are given under respective sub-headings.

Chronological CV #2

This is a more typical example of this type of résumé, with the objective and USP at the top, followed by the evidence a) in support of the objective and b) to expand upon and add proof to the USP. Having progressed through the ranks at various firms, he has decided to gel all his experience in manufacturing to have sole responsibility for a full site.

Functional CV #1

I included this example to illustrate how even a graduate with little work experience can shine.

Functional CV #2

Our example in this case has been a bit directionless, but still manages to make a coherent picture out of his work history. From a business course, he started out in production management and then moved into engineering sales to broaden his scope. However, he missed the promotional boat, so he switched to more lucrative medical sales. Being not to his tastes, he flitted about for three years, having three different sales jobs, only the most significant of which being mentioned here. He now wishes to combine his past jobs by getting into engineering sales management.

Combined CV #1

This CV lists an impressive array of successes, which would otherwise look dis-jointed and, due to the frequent changes in job title, be somewhat hidden in a work history format. It also masks 8-months unemployment in 1991 due to a site closure. In 1990, he says he was design project leader. There may well have been 3 or 4 such project leaders, all working on different products, but this is astutely omitted.

Combined CV #2

This person wants to add to her experience in clothing retail. Although a little limited, there are again some impressive figures to be highlighted, which are listed first. Two years in kitchenware is too long to be ignored and so has to be included. As it is now at the very bottom, it will be by-the-by, compared to the impressive list of achievements gone before. There is also subtle use of funny money here. The second accomplishment says increased margins by 50%. An increase of 10% to 15% is only a difference of 5%, arithmetically, but it is still an increase of 50% – a far more impressive figure. Notice also the way in which the job of least note is presented: "promoted from section supervisor". There may be nothing to talk about in this job which is relevant to being a prestigious clothier, but this simple sentence both explains the year's gap at the bottom and does it by way of the most useful word which came out of this job: promotion.

Chronological #1

Marianne Dyson

12, Basingstoke Road, Plumpton, Cambridge, CB10 2RJ
Home: 0123 645 1313   e-mail: mari@mirage.net

Objective: Principal vaccine researcher in a small bio-tech company.

Key Abilities
- Accomplished Researcher and Laboratory Technician.
- 6 years experience as a laboratory technician, working on various vaccines.
- 3 years vaccine research experience.
- Presented 16 papers at seminars and training programs in U.K. and U.S.
- Analysed economic conditions, business trends and potential markets for vaccines.

Employment

Research Associate,   **Jan. 1997 to Present**
Bio-synth Laboratories, Cambridge.
Principal associate to Dr. Maxwell Raul, Ph.D. on vaccine project with £20m annual sales potential. Sent as company representative to six international conferences. Presented papers at 1998 and 1999 London conferences.

Laboratory Technician,   **Aug. 1991 to Jan. 1997**
Bio-synth, Laboratories, Cambridge.
Specialised in research project under the supervision of Val Seymour, Ph.D. Co-wrote research papers presented at the UK Biochemical Research AGMs.

Articles Published

- "The Pharmacokinetics of Inert Chemicals and Their Relation to Vaccines in Humans." *Presented at the IVRS 45th Congress, London, March 13, 1994.* J.D. Gordon, M.D., L.L. Sharma, Ph.D., March 1999.   *...etc...*

Education

PhD, Biochemistry, New College, Cambridge   June 1996
Specialisation in Pharmaceutical Chemistry.

B.Sc. Chemistry, Leeds University   June 1991
Additional courses in pharmaceutical science and chemical engineering.

References: Available on request.

Chronological #2

Michael Hathersage
48, Cherrytree Road, Prestwich, Manchester, M25 2SD
Home 0161 737 9680   mike.hathers@mirage.net

OBJECTIVE
Site manager of a small manufacturing firm.

SUMMARY
10 years of significant achievement through production management to productivity consultant. Principal abilities in strategic and operational analysis, productivity improvement, training and production planning.

CAREER PROFILE
Productivity Consultant, 1997 - 2000
TolTec Business Consultants
3 years of realising significant bottom-line improvements through strategic alignment, productivity and management system analysis and employee training. Clients include Allied Chemicals, Seymore Engineering and Northern Distribution.

Production Manager, 1994 - 1997
Turnpike Automotive, Warrington, Manchester
Directed £2m up-grade of production facility. Rationalised product mix and operating procedures to achieve £1.2m annual saving. Initiated continuous improvement programme and team-working procedures.

Production Manager, 1992-1994
Hall Engineering Ltd., Preston, Lancashire
Managed 80 personnel in 2 departments. Installed new planning system and devised employee training programme. Improved productivity by 22%, reduced downtime by 18% and maintenance costs by 15%.

Shift Manager, 1990 - 1992
Red Rose Engineering Steels Ltd., Bolton, Lancashire
Project leader to optimise work scheduling. Reduced downtime by 20%. Wrote BS5750 quality documents.

EDUCATION   B.Eng. (Hons.) Production and Operations Management
University of Lancashire (1988).

REFERENCES   Available on request.

44

Functional #1

Siobhan Williams
160, Chatteray Road, Salisbury, Wiltshire
Home: 01254 773 0681 e-mail: shiobhan@mirage.net

Position Desired: Technical Writer

Summary of Qualifications

- B.Eng. (Hons.), Chemical engineering.
- Member of Bristol Writer's Guild.
- Associate member of the Institute of Chemical Engineers.
- Authored 2 full specification manuals, 1 sales manual, 1 corporate Web page and several information documents, during work placements.

Skills and Abilities

- Efficient, accurate, and detail-oriented.
- Strong written and verbal communication skills.
- Transcription and proof-reading experience (60wpm, 10-key).
- Fluent with MS Office, Adobe PageMaker, MS FrontPage, Harvard graphics and Macintosh.

Education

1996- 2000   **B.Eng. (Hons.), Chemical engineering, Class 2:1**
         University of Bristol
Final year project to construct a sales manual for Pura Chemicals filtration and purification model FS201 for off-shore use. Intermediate year at Pura Chemicals authoring promotional material for annual trade shows. Created company's first Web site.

1996   **A-Levels:** Computer science, English, Business studies.

References   Available on request.

Functional #2

Greg Goldsmith
25, Hammond Road, Newcastle
<u>Home</u>: 0131 255 2525, <u>Mobile:</u> 07774 2803210
<u>e-mail</u>: greg@mirage.net

Objective
Engineering sales management position with accountability for objectives and growth.

Summary
- 8 years sales and manufacturing experience.
- Specialist in high-tech sales, market development and sales management.
- Proven performer with demonstrated ability to gain account loyalty and win preferential supply agreements.
- Excellent rapport-building, presentation, and closing skills.
- Merchandised the most profitable line in the company.

Experience
Sales Executive, Castle EMS, 1997-2000
North of England field sales of electronic, microscopic and spectroscopic analysis equipment. Secured new contracts valued at £500k per year.

Medical Sales Representative, MediStore Inc., 1995-1996
General medical sales in the north-east sector. Introduced market-penetration techniques that realised 27% increase in business in 9 months.

Field Sales Executive, Alpha Medical Monitors, 1994 – 1995
Secured 5-year supply deal with largest customer. Secured total of £600k of new business.

Cell leader, Alpha Medical Monitors, 1992 - 1994
Managed the production, quality and cost control of medical monitoring equipment, liaising with design and field sales.

Education   B.Sc., Economics and Business Studies (1989)
                  University of the Bath

References   Available on request.

Combined #1

Chris McInlay
28, Forth Avenue, Dumbarton, Glasgow, G62 2YA
<u>Home</u>: 0121 789 1234   <u>e-mail</u>: chris.mac@mirage.net

Objective
Site Manager of an SME in furniture manufacturing.

Accomplishments
1999   Turned £3m annual loss into £10m profit within 2 years at 125-employee furniture manufacturing site.

1996   Promoted to site manager following successful re-organisation of national sales teams, cutting costs by 17% and man-power by 9% (re-assigned to new business-development team).

1994   Increased northern region business by 20% in 2 years as regional sales manager.

1990   Successfully launched new range of office furniture as design project leader.

1986   B.Sc. (Hons.) Materials Science.

Career History
1997 – present   Site Manager, Lomond Office Furniture, Glasgow.
Initiated kaisen practice, rationalised product mix and re-organised shop-floor to dovetail with new sales structure. Reduced wastage by £90k p.a., re-work by 200k, improved productivity by 19%, sales increased by 5%.

1992 – 1997 Sales Mgr (North) Lomond Office Furniture, Glasgow.
Re-organised sales team to reflect customer profile, rather than product mix. Project leader in applying this system to other regions.

1989 – 1991 Design technician, Signature Offices.
Project leader in design of ergonomic, individual multi-media desks.

1986 – 1989 Design technician, Signature Offices.
CAD design technician for bespoke office installations.

Education
B.Sc. (Hons.) Materials Eng'g & Design, University of Nott'm (1986).

References   Available on request

Combined #2

Paula Hanson
37 Pottery Way, Stoke-on-Trent, Staffordshire, ST12 2DD
Home: 01542 277 8978   e-mail: paula@mirage.net

OBJECTIVE   Retail management position in a prestigious clothiers.

SUMMARY OF QUALIFICATIONS
6 years retail management experience, including high-profile, city centre outlets.
* Successful market positioning of previously managed stores.
* Proficient in planning and budgeting; employee training and motivation; adherence to company standards and policies; customer relations; expense and invisible waste control.

ACCOMPLISHMENTS
2000   Re-aligned clothing store to premier city outlet, increasing profits by 80% in less than 2 years.
1997   Increased turn-over by 250% and margins by 50% at newly relocated store.
1996   Relocated clothing store to primary city-centre location of 4,000 square feet, from secondary location of 800 square feet, within first year of employment as store manager.
1995   Average 10% year-to-year sales increase as department manager.

EXPERIENCE
Store Manager, Paul Mattier Clothiers, Chester   1997 to Present
Converted merchandise presentation from budget/moderate to upscale. Reduced inventory level and expanded accessory areas to complete total presentation. Full responsibility for business profitability.

Store Manager, Interstate Clothing, Stoke   1995 to 1997
Re-configured merchandise from teen to twenties C1, C2 s/e group. Re-located store to prime city-centre location.

Housewares Department Manager   1993 to 1995
Kitchen equipment. Promoted from section supervisor. Responsible for layout and up-keep of 2000 item displays.

EDUCATION   **B.A., Marketing**   1992, Chester Polytechnic.

REFERENCES   Available on request

4

The Cover Letter

The cover letter, though often woefully neglected, can play an integral part in getting you an interview. Despite all your hard work thus far, you are still risking being on a loser if the cover letter does not inspire the reader to look further. If the letter is not enticing enough or doesn't promote interest in you, your skills, your abilities and your experiences, then the reader will be biased against whatever may be in the body of the CV. Their expectation will be low, and people generally conclude what they expect.

Too often the cover letter is written simply as a letter, with two or three paragraphs of text telling the reader what they are, or have been, doing and that they are now looking for a new job. For a start, block text is not inviting to read, especially when you have several dozen to get through. Secondly, all such stuff is on the CV anyway, in an easier to read format. Instead, the letter should be a succinct summation of your key qualifications and qualities; essentially your USP.

When you get junk mail in the post, you will often see what's called 'teaser copy' on the envelope. This is supposed to get you excited about the contents of the envelope and have you ripping it open in expectation. Unfortunately, most direct mail of this nature is just garbage. Big, colourful lettering, gaudy graphics, company logos and things in the envelope that move, all immediately yell out to you, "Junk Mail! Quick, throw me away." However, done properly, the teaser copy will be a direct reflection of the headline inside, with insinuations as to the major benefits of reading further. This is the form your cover letter should take.

There are many forms of cover letter, depending whether you are cold-calling, responding to an advert or working your network. Examples of letters you may need to use at some stage in your job search are on the following pages.

They can all take a similar format, to keep them concise, benefit-ridden and to the point. Using this format, your letter should alter little regardless of your situation. Whether you are job switching, re-entering the job market or career changing, you will need to identify the requirements of your target post and company and apply your most appropriate benefits to that. If you have been away for a while, you may, if appropriate, have to point out how you have kept your skills sharp.

The most difficult application is the speculative one, where you cold-call via letter to a firm of your choosing. You could write hundreds of these without result. You are far better off sticking to the channels discussed in chapter 6. Even if you are re-locating, it would be much more productive to follow these other options than to write on spec. You can also ask a newsagent in the area to send you a copy of the job-day regional paper.

Below are a few examples of cover letters, including one related to a previous example and one I used to use myself.

The first I have used to illustrate how a response to an advert should look. It is derived from Combined CV #1, provided earlier. By picking out the few major selling points, it appears at first read like this person has had a solid, successful, progressive career, whereas in fact it has been somewhat dis-jointed. This example is the minimum content I would suggest.

The second is the body of a letter I used to use myself. I would further recommend your letter be no longer than this one. My own 'career' wasn't so much a career as a progressive series of jobs in the manufacturing sector. Yet it was still possible to extract the most relevant points and mould them around the job description. To do this, I first listed in bullet form my own achievements. Then, under 'synthesis', I listed what this meant to the employer. Each line was the proof of satisfaction of one of the stipulated job requirements from the advert. Using this technique, my response rate went from pitiful to around 20-25%. That gave me lots of interview practice and landed me a job in around half the time normally expected. This was for a general manager-type position.

Response to an advert

This is the commonest one. This is how I recommend your cover letter should look.

Chris McInlay
28, Forth Avenue, Dumbarton, Glasgow, G62, 2YA
Home: 0121 789 1234   *e-mail*: chris.mac@mirage.net

BetterCo.
Victory Road
Glasgow, G45

21 October, 2000

Site Manager (ref. SC23/00)

Dear Mr. Smith,

I refer to your recent advertisement for the above position. In response to the criteria of the position, I consider myself suitable in respect of the following:

- 14 years total experience in furniture manufacturing, including site manager, regional sales and CAD design.

- Turned £3m annual loss into £10m profit within 2 years as manager of 125-employee furniture manufacturing site.

- Proven history of generating profitability and of increasing sales.

I would welcome the opportunity to discuss with you further the promising fit between your requirements and my experience and abilities.

Sincerely,

Chris McInlay

Enc.: résumé

(Contact details)

Monday, 23rd February, 1992

General Manager (ref. M23/92)

Dear Mr. Smith,

I refer to your recent advertisement for the above position. In response to the criteria of the position, I consider myself suitable in respect of the following:

- Seven years in manufacturing management and consultancy.
- Primary experience in production management, productivity improvement and quality issues.
- B. Eng. (Hons.) and MBA.
- Wealth of knowledge on management systems and productivity analysis techniques.
- Considerable experience of solo- and team-project leadership.
- Proficient with many popular computer packages.

Synthesis

- Extensive operational experience at all levels.
- Highly experienced man-manager.
- Successful application of productivity improvement issues, continuous improvement and change management.
- Well-developed inter-personal and communication skills from shop-floor to board level.
- Experienced in the theory and practice of the identification, analysis and solution of business issues.
- Familiar with ISO 9002, BS5750, SPC, TQM and general quality issues.
- Experienced and effective presenter.

I would very much welcome the opportunity to discuss with you the promising fit between my background and qualifications and the requirements of the position.

Sincerely,

Signature

The job description in this latter one, as is usual, wanted someone who could turn around flagging fortunes, team-build and improve quality. So that became the focus of my points. I included the communication and presentations skills bit because I assumed that explanation and persuasion would be key parts to winning through with new ideas. I'd also done my fair share, so I was in no fear of being shown up if they asked me to prove it.

You'll notice a lack of figures here. In this case, I had done so many different jobs, extracting even the best figures would be a dilution of the overall message. Instead, I kept to my USP of seven years of manufacturing management and related to the key job requirements. On reflection, though, I would have replaced the word 'proficient' (in computers) with 'fluent'. Actually, I thought I was a complete duffer, but compared to most of the people I encountered, I turned out to be a bit of a whizz. No match for the pros, but not bad amongst your average paper-pushers. So, again, it's how you are perceived that counts. Even if you turn out to be not as fluent as you thought, it's a genuine enough mistake to make.

Oh, and don't worry too much about the opening sentence, it won't get read anyway. That's why my own was so short. Here's another closing sentence I used which, either by luck or judgement, got a better response than most:

"I believe this position will allow me to fully gel my experiences and abilities to date and precipitate real benefit for your organisation. I would very much welcome the opportunity to discuss this with you further."

The key phrase here is "benefit to your organisation". To paraphrase JFK, it's not what they can do for you, but what you can do for them. Now let's take a brief look at some other letters you may have to consider in the course of your job hunt.

The Follow-up Letter

These are supposedly intended to re-express your interest in a post after the interview. Some people will heartily recommend this as a point of courtesy that can swing the odds in your favour. This is largely wishful thinking. As we shall see in future chapters, your fate in interview will have been decided in the first few minutes, almost certainly by the end of the interview and definitely by the time your letter reaches them – or, at least, it should have done if they know what they're looking for. You should clinch the deal in the interview itself and not have to go crawling back afterwards, taking up more of their time and appearing a little desperate.

I wouldn't therefore recommend it. But if you just can't hold yourself back then you should:

- Thank them for seeing you;
- Tell them what particular points from your discussions interested you;
- Restate your USP;
- Remind them which of your key skills and abilities would particularly suit or solve the business issues you have mentioned thus far in your letter.

The Networking Letter

This is where you wish to approach a new contact, to whom you may well be of benefit. You may be looking to change careers and are looking for advice or for other contacts; or you could have got wind of a vacancy through someone you know; or you could even have identified a company that could use your particular expertise.

It is important to get the tone right in these letters. It should be short and to the point, but with sufficient detail to arouse interest in the reader. It should be assertive, but not demanding; polite, but not creepy. And, where relevant, it should mention your contact's name and the reason for getting in touch. A couple of examples are given below.

You should always include a copy of your résumé. If you have targeted your letter correctly (and your contact information is true) and you succeed in sparking some interest in your reader, he or she will want to know more. Note that, in each example letter, the introduction is again short and then it gets right into promising benefits to the reader. The bullet points listed should be your USP and principal benefits, viewed from your prospect's point of view.

In these cases, it is also important to include a 'call to action'. You have contacted them because it could be mutually beneficial, and they wouldn't want to miss that, would they? So you let them know that you will be contacting them in due course. Give them a few days grace to get something together and perhaps set a time aside, but don't leave it too long or they will forget about you or assume that it is not that urgent or important.

These letters are in my own particular style, which you may not like. It is important, though, not to be too apologetic since any result will be mutually beneficial. Conversely, you don't want to appear a tad arrogant or pushy.

Jane Davenport
City Insurance
Wrexham

23rd April, 1999

Dear Ms. Davenport,

If you will excuse the unsolicited approach, I am writing under the advice of a colleague, (name, position), who suggested that my expertise would be of benefit to you.

Currently I am personnel officer at TolTec Engineering. I have elected to switch into insurance in order to dedicate my skills to a company that offers longer-term prospects. My relevant credentials would be:

- 7 years total office experience.
  - 3 years as secretary to regional sales manager.
  - 4 years administrative experience, including paper and computer record maintenance.
- 50wpm typing speed.
- Fluent in many popular computer packages.

Perhaps we could arrange a meeting to discuss how I may be of use to your organisation. I will call your office within the next few days to confirm a suitable time.

Sincerely,

Signature

Ron Schneider
TriDim Marketing
Cradley Heath
Birmingham

1st March, 1998

Dear Mr. Schneider,

As the (job position) of one of the most renowned companies in the high-tech marketing industry, I would be most grateful if you could spare a few moments to advise me on how to enter your particular field.

I am seeking to progress into marketing consultancy with a high-tech bias, to apply my skills to more progressive and lucrative business sectors. My credentials are:

* B.A. (Hons.) in Economics and Business Studies (1989).
* M.A. Marketing (1992).
* 4 years business-to-business marketing experience.
* 3 years commercial marketing experience.

I would appreciate any advice or assistance you may have. If it is convenient, perhaps you would care for a lunch appointment. I will contact your secretary within the next few days to arrange a suitable time.

Thank you for taking the time to read this letter.

Sincerely,

Signature

Henry Senior
Bespoke Strategies, Inc.
Sheffield

3rd May, 1999

Dear Mr. Senior,

I am writing under the advice of a common acquaintance, (name, position), who suggested that my expertise would be of particular benefit to your organisation.

I am currently business analyst at ProMark Systems, Ltd. (Name) informs me, in confidence, that your business expansion plans may require the skills that I possess and have demonstrated to good effect over the past 3 years. I have enclosed my résumé to illustrate. In summary, I have:

- 3 years experience in market analysis and business forecasting techniques.
- The ability to speedily quantify optimum business supply profiles and dovetail these with market trends.
- B.Sc. Economics and Applied Mathematics.
- Fluent with Microsoft Office and other packages.

Perhaps we could arrange a meeting to discuss how I may be of use to your organisation. I will call your office within the next few days to confirm a suitable time.

Sincerely,

Signature

Notice in the first letter the phrase "dedicate my skills to". This puts the emphasis of "a switch into insurance" as a benefit for the company, rather than a personal benefit. As the saying goes, "it's the thought that counts" and this sends the correct empathetic message. Clearly, the "longer-term prospects" is the personal side that creates the balance.

You should be able to explain why you believe there are better prospects in insurance and why you have chosen this field in particular. Perhaps you have evidence of long tenure and good employee policies in this sector. Perhaps your current situation simply couldn't be any worse. And no doubt you have friends in the industry who can increase your learning curve (another benefit for the company).

The second letter gives no indication that you could be looking for a job at TriDim, though this may actually be the case. To do this may be too direct and put people on the back foot. If your belief that there are opportunities at TriDim turns out to be true, you can bet your boots your contact will be sizing you up at your meeting without you even implying that you want in.

The third letter, however, does have a direct approach. A post has been flagged at Bespoke and you have got wind of it. So there is no harm in indicating your intentions here.

One further reason why the cover letter can be so important is that everybody has their own ideas about how a CV should look. Certain layouts will be more appealing to certain people. By following the above examples, there can be little room for personal judgement. If the reader has decided to turn to your CV from the letter, there is something about you that they are keen to read up on. The appearance of your CV, although it may not be their personal ideal version, will be secondary to finding what they are now looking for. Your sales pitch is working.

Now let's take a look at the job market itself to see how to apply these new-found skills to the job hunt itself. As always, there is a degree of preparation to be done, starting with understanding the nature of the job market and the kind of approach we need to adopt in order to succeed.

5

Business Realities And The Self-Managed Career Path

The nature of job hunting and career progression has changed radically in recent years. The way in which recruitment and development is approached is gradually catching up. Enlightened businesses retain their best employees by giving the support and development the individual needs, rather than applying blanket organisational training programmes. In addition, the 'hard', structured, criteria-defined, textbook approach is fading in favour of the 'softer' side. In a nutshell, the 'hard' approach is defined, instructional, written, specified; the 'soft' approach is personal, inter-personal, cognitive, non-quantifiable.

So, to be useful to you personally, it would therefore be inappropriate to lay down recipes, formulae or lists of things to do, to tick off as you go, which would claim to bring you to a fabulous job at the end of the day. That is the blanket approach. Instead, what you will find here, is an array of ideas, concepts and techniques that, if you apply them properly, will put you at a real and lasting advantage in today's employment arena. As such, you will find the next two chapters not to be overly instructional; more advice-oriented.

It should be stressed at this point that career planning is a personal venture. You can scan every journal, newspaper and magazine, enlist everyone you know, network all you like and visit every agency in the land. But the only person with your interests firmly at heart, the only one with the time and the will, with the grit to fight rejection, with the persistence and the vision…is you. Add to that the increasing necessity to improve on the softer elements of job hunting and you see how subjective this selling process is. For that is what job hunting is – a selling process: you 'sell' (i.e. market) yourself to prospective employers.

This means you must be fully conversant with your product (you), the benefits of your product to your customers (what you can do for them) and how best to present this product and these benefits. This book is intended to enable you to do just that – but only if you are prepared to do the necessary work to assess and analyse your product and to work on its presentation. I would advise you at this point to keep an open mind concerning whether or not you believe you already have a clear career path in mind and be prepared to do some thinking – the hardest thinking of all: objective and predictive.

Let me elaborate with a moment's existentialism! The only way we are similar is that we're all different. Everybody is wired up differently according to his or her own genetics, upbringing, experiences, abilities, rationale and emotions. Now that's quite a list of fairly hefty parameters. So, focusing on the matter in hand – job hunting and career planning – you have to understand yourself, your situation, your skills, your aspirations, your potential and your goals and then adapt the principals we will be covering to suit your own situation. As Tennyson wrote: "Self-reverence, self-knowledge and self-control. These three alone lead life to sovereign power." Don't take prescriptions; absorb and adapt, then apply your own decisions.

Trouble is, most people are not used to thinking for themselves, particularly in an objective manner. For it is not easy. Many spend more time planning their next shopping trip than they do their careers or the rest of their lives. They wait to be told what their next pay rise will be, whether they will be required on a project, what their objectives for next year are – if they're lucky enough to get such – what their next job will be and even if they will have one this time next year.

For you, though, this is great. For while the majority of people are dangling from the puppet strings of their organisation in the ever-changing set of the corporate theatre, you are writing your own script to suit the mood of the audience. An audience which, for you, comprises a whole array of employers from a variety of business sectors.

Over the next few chapters, you will be equipping yourself with the ability to make your own career decisions as and when you see fit, rather than when circumstances require. You will be able to define your own self-managed career path, free from market vagaries and free from reliance on any one organisation.

We will look at the traits, tricks and techniques you should be giving serious consideration to in order to survive and prosper in today's job market. Then you need to <u>adapt</u> these to your own situation and your own goals.

We will first cover what the modern job market is all about (if you hadn't already figured it for yourself!); what attitude you need to adopt in order to prosper and how to develop that attitude into a way of working life. At the end, you should be ready to go into business – as yourself and for yourself. Not as an employee, but as a marketable commodity. One that goes to the highest bidder and to the one that is prepared to fund your goals. Let me just re-emphasise that previous point:

You're Not An Employee, You're A Marketable Commodity.

This is a central theme which we will be returning to. For now, throw away those old ideas of company loyalty, of the psychological contract, of company development programmes, and especially of a fair day's work. For one thing is for sure – life ain't fair. You just have to swing the odds in your favour. Apply the advice in this book and you'll stand a pretty good chance of coming up trumps. We are not out to buck any trends here; we are aiming to key into actual market developments and to capitalise on them so that <u>you</u> may benefit.

The job market is gearing up towards employee independence (if that isn't too much of a contradiction in terms!). This transformation in the nature of organisations is a complex and involving study of the tapestry of social, economic and political threads, inter-woven across the years. But understanding the nature of modern organisations is important in realising the directly associated nature of job hunting and career development. I will try to give a concise account of these changes so you may more clearly realise the validity of the strategies advocated here and so apply them with confidence.

In the 20th century, organisations went through a number of transformations. At the turn of the century, the individual industrialists predominated, growing into large internationals (Siemens, Ford, Lever, Sumitomo). Pre-WWII, the scientific managers revolutionised the workplace through job analysis, breaking it down into it's elements and describing and organising these elements for greatest productivity. This saw the birth of the management organisation, required to monitor, control, instruct and apply the necessary resources for the completion of the work. Thus the worker was made slave to the process: analysis determined the nature of the job, the sequence of operation and indeed the speed of the worker.

We have now gone beyond management. Valued productivity no longer derives from the allocation of capital, labour and resources, as with the traditional role of management. Productivity now comes from the application of <u>knowledge</u> and in the performance of knowledge. The most valuable knowledge is therefore in the hands of the specialist: the market expert, the software engineer, the statistician, the business analyst, the designer and so on. The generalists are no longer the most productive contributors; the specialist "knowledge workers" are the most valuable.

The term "knowledge worker" was coined by Peter Drucker in his 1994 book, "Post Capitalist Society". This elucidative study of modern business realities is probably too complex to be understood by an initiate of organisational studies. As a minimum introduction to this field, I would first suggest reading the following two texts:

"The Practice of Management", Peter F. Drucker (Butterworth-
    Heinemann, 1954);
"Understanding Organisations", Charles Handy (Penguin, 1993).

Don't be put off by the first one dating back to 1954. This remarkable work contains many theories and predictions on successful management practice which, though some may now be considered basic, many firms consistently fail to implement to this day.

To continue, the successful management of knowledge workers demands a recognition and appreciation of their talents and a nurturing of their knowledge that feeds this talent. Drucker likens the new organisation to a symphony orchestra. You will not find lead violin playing bassoon on occasion. Nor does any one member by themselves create music and no one contribution is any more valuable than another. So rewards between the contributors should not vary – certainly a trend in successful "flat" organisations (see chapter 6). Clearly, under this analogy, it is not worth having a first rate string section and a third rate brass section: the collective effort is reduced to the lowest common denominator. Only when focused towards a common goal does the collective effort create a piece worthy of an audience.

"This means", says Drucker, "organisations have to market membership. They have to attract people, hold people, recognise and reward people, motivate people, serve and satisfy people. Because the knowledge organisation is an organisation of specialists, it has to be an organisation of equals, of colleagues, of associates. No knowledge 'ranks' higher than any other. The position of each is determined by the contribution to the common task, rather than by any inherent superiority or inferiority."

A principal difference between traditional (and decreasing) workers and knowledge workers is that the latter own the means of production. Take particular note of the word 'own'. In the modern organisation, the tools of production are worthless without the application of the knowledge of the knowledge worker. The computer is a prime example. This machine only operates at the speed and efficiency of its operator – the opposite of the case in the management organisation. The use of information, an increasingly valuable commodity, is another case in point. Successful rapid assimilation and exploitation of information can provide a powerful competitive advantage. And that is the domain of the knowledge worker.

For the modern employee, then, organisations are your market. Gaining access to them allows you to apply your knowledge (i.e. sell your wares) and to generate profit (an income) by satisfying a need within the organisation for your particular talents. If there are more lucrative markets for you to apply to, then you are free to compete there also, against other knowledge workers. You are, in effect, self-employed. This is a subject we will return to in chapter 6 from a different, personal-development angle, rather than a purely business-reality angle.

Some of the issues we will be covering may be familiar to you, others not. Some you may disagree with. But like I said, it's up to you to act on these ideas and principals and adapt them to your own cause. If you choose not to, you stand a better chance of remaining susceptible to the ebb and flow of business fortune and of being swept away in shifting tides. Instead, you can be a well-equipped, sea-worthy vessel, powered by your own steam and guided by your own map and compass.

Let's begin by looking at some of the central principals which will develop your confidence and ability when pursuing your own self-managed career path and so give you the freedom of the job market.

Developing A Winning Attitude

Winning is an often mis-used term. To be meaningful, it should be a relative measure. Relative to what? Well, consider this. Would an athlete who refrained from turning professional just so he could keep winning races be regarded as a winner? Having failed to fulfil his potential as a professional athlete, he would most likely be regarded as a bit of a failure, even though he consistently wins his races. So winning is not the opposite of losing in an absolute sense; it is relative to our own potential.

The term 'loser', on the other hand, is most often used as a rather derogatory term, as a means to gain a sense of one-up-manship over someone less fortunate. Those who seek to pick on 'losers' as some pathetic little ego-trip are not actually doing anything themselves that would allow them to be called winners. And that is an essential trait of a real loser: a blip in someone else's efforts is seized upon in a vain attempt to elevate themselves. In reality, they make no personal improvement at all.

Similarly, on a business level, the way to fall behind is to stand still. If you do nothing to improve or to progress, then you will lose. If you want to get ahead, you have to try new things, different things, risky things. To err in your efforts does not make you a loser; it is how you learn, grow and evolve. What other traits can be gleaned from the above example that point to the traits of a winner?

1. Don't compare yourself to others.

Comparison is the fast track to misery. In fact it can be positively evil. It can lead to all sorts of bigotry and hatred. On a lighter note, we typically see it at work in 'the principal of social comparison'. This says that you would be perfectly happy with your rewards in life until you discover what your friends are getting. Even if they are in totally unrelated fields, have worked harder than you, have made braver decisions and perhaps suffered in the process – it still just ain't fair! But they get up at six in the morning, suffer undue pressure and risk redundancy at any moment! Yeah, but 15 grand more!! Lucky swine. Even if your mate gets a 5% pay rise and you get 2%, you are resentful, despite the fact you get 5 more holiday days than she does.

The key is to assess yourself against your own abilities and goals and gauge how fulfilled you feel. If you're going to compare anything, compare everything. Perhaps your partner is not a Page 3 or a Chippendale, but at least they don't cheat on you. You may not be the brightest lamp in the street, but at least you don't sulk all day and ruin your home life if you don't get your way. Nevertheless, it is best not to compare at all. Be aware of when you are doing this.

2. Be willing to take risks.

This is a major quality of a winner. As pointed out above, you don't get anywhere by not taking risks. Trundle along in your happy, content, safe little rut and that's where you'll stay. Just about everyone has heard the Thomas Edison story. It took him over two thousand attempts to succeed in creating the light bulb. When asked what kept him going after two thousand failures, he replied had not failed at all, but that he had *discovered* two thousand ways *not* to make a bulb.

The key is to frame your failures in a positive light (if you pardon the pun). Assess your approach, pin down your mistakes, learn from them, then re-adjust and re-focus for the future.

You won't get everything right all the time. You *will* make mistakes and have failures. What we are looking for here is controlled risk. By way of analogy, you know that jumping out of a perfectly good aircraft at 5,000 feet will always carry some risk. But with the appropriate kit and some good training, you're pretty certain you can land on your feet. Likewise, you don't want to risk a sound livelihood on a whim, a notion or someone else's unsubstantiated say so. You must do your research first, get informed, trained, practiced and then go for it. The more you dig and the more you assess and analyse, the less uncertain will be your 'risk'.

3. Continue doing the same things and you'll get the same results.

To keep repeating the same behaviours whilst expecting a different result is a pretty good definition of insanity. A couple of examples will help illustrate this point, one simple, one less obvious.

The guy next door to me has a blue tit box about four feet off the ground. Every year, some or all of the chicks are lost to cats. He's "tried everything" to protect them: a metal framework underneath and on top, keeping a vigil, cutting the surrounding shrubs back so there are less places for the cats to hide, greasing the top so they can't get a purchase. Everything, that is, except moving the box! Nothing else would be a problem if the box were higher up. This is the real issue. This is the thing he must do differently. It's not the shrubs or the box construction or even the cats themselves. Raise the box and all other problems would go away.

Here's another, trickier, but more relevant one. For most of my employed career, I was in manufacturing. Every year, I experienced redundancy. For the first few years I escaped; whenever I moved job within the firm, pretty soon that previous job disappeared. I felt I was being hunted. Eventually I took voluntary redundancy. From then on, I moved *company* every year, sometimes after only a few months. Every time I thought I was learning a bit more about the game and how to survive. But every year was the same. I knew about this rule and I thought I was applying it. What on earth was I doing wrong? Finally it dawned: "Get the hell out of manufacturing!" Obvious really – but not when you're on the inside. And this is the problem of subjectivity. I was going from one manufacturing firm to another and expecting it to get better when manufacturing had been in decline for over two decades. My 'box' wasn't my approach or my training or my qualifications, it was manufacturing and I wasn't looking outside of it. I had the choice of job-switching, re-training or going it alone. As you can see, I chose the latter.

4. Take 100% responsibility.

Put simply, quit complaining and quit blaming others. If you're late for work, leave earlier – don't blame the traffic. If you hate your work, don't blame the boss, get a different job (see No.2!). *Your* response to any situation is what determines the outcome, not what others do or say. Losers always blame the <u>event</u> for things going wrong, never their response to that event. And then they continue their typical responses expecting the event, or the outcome to the event, to be different this time around (see 3). Winners realise that it is up to them and them alone if they want the outcome to be to their liking, so they tweak their response to the event to influence that outcome.

You can practice this in any part of your life. Instead of fighting external influences and getting nowhere, consider the options <u>you</u> can take to alter the outcome. Consider my own situation above. I could easily have continued to blame my redundancies on business failure from poor management. However true it might have been, it was doing me no good. Instead, I changed tack: I turned away from manufacturing.

A drastic example, but it works equally in everyday situations. Instead of badgering someone to do something, try humouring them or playing the guilt card, explaining how difficult they are making things for you. If you're forever forgetting or mislaying things, make lists, get key-hooks, storage trays, files and boxes. Always look for the different approach *you* can take to change the outcome, rather than trying to alter the event or alter other people's behaviour.

5. Winners are happy to experience discomfort.

To step outside of your comfort zone, to try new events or new responses and to experience new outcomes is uncomfortable. To do this sometimes requires risk – even more discomforting. To foul up and to suffer the fall out is worse still. But to try new things and to learn from your mistakes is how you grow. You need to keep your eye on the goal and have the will and self-belief to sustain yourself through it all – something we'll come back to later. It's all too easy to sit in your comfort zone and watch the world go by. That's for losers.

If you got any of those points, you have real potential to be a Winner. It's no simple option, mind. Adapting these traits is a life-long learning experience, but it's something you can do every day. And this is as important as any of the above traits. We don't move forward in great leaps and bounds, but by taking small, incremental steps. A little application and a little progression each and every day. Let's summarise:

Trait 1: Never compare yourself to others.
Trait 2: Take risks if you want to progress.
Trait 3: Change your response to situations to get the result that suits you.
Trait 4: Take 100% responsibility for everything that happens in your life.
Trait 5: Be willing to step out of your comfort zone.

I don't want to dwell too much on these points because this is a career-planning book, not a self-help seminar. These traits, though, will have a very real relevance to your success over the coming years in planning your own career – and, of course, in taking action to secure it. A plan means nothing if it is not acted upon. And to implement your plan, you will need to develop the above qualities. They are critical for you to gain control of your own career development – effective, growth-oriented control.

However, when whole organisations can fail to appreciate these traits, it is not surprising that those dangling from their corporate strings also follow suit. Let us paraphrase an example situation at some mythical company, StoneAge, Inc., to highlight the point. It might go something like this:

"Profits are down again. What are we going to do?"
"We need to address our profitability."
"Yeah, but from what angle?"

"BetterCo implemented a TQM program last year and saw a 10% increase in profit."
"By doing what exactly?"
"All the workforce brainstorm the problems they see and then they implement what they reckon to be the best solution...basically."
"Oh, do they indeed? Well, let's have some of that then."

It's a simplified but common enough scenario. Let's assess some of the flaws in the theory.

For a start, who's to say that BetterCo's profit increase was due to their TQM program and not, say, to new products, a newly acquired subsidiary or altered accounting practices? Who's to say that the workforce at StoneAge is going to open up and respond to management requests? BetterCo may have much better industrial relations than StoneAge. Who knows if the problems at StoneAge are similar to those at BetterCo? Do StoneAge's management have the open-mindedness to run with a TQM program? And so on.

But the biggest mistake of all is assuming that just because it worked for BetterCo, it is going to work for StoneAge as well. To get all academic for a minute, the 'law of biological exclusivity' says that there is only room for one species in any environment. If there are two, there will be competition. One will win and the other will either die or move on. Companies are organisms like any other. They exist because there is a market need to satisfy. This is their food. The firm evolves a physiology (operations structure, financial structure, marketing style, logistical framework and so on) to make consumption of that food as efficient as possible; i.e. within it's territory, it sells to the market in the most efficient and profitable manner it can devise. As soon as another firm muscles in on it's food source, battle will commence. Even if there is food a-plenty, one will grow at the expense of the other. As a result, every organisation sits in its own particular micro- (or macro-) environment and is therefore unique. Unique in either the market it supplies, the nature of the customers it serves, in its management style and structure, in its operations and so on. So BetterCo and StoneAge will, by definition, be two different entities. BetterCo's solutions will not lay comfortably over StoneAge's problems.

So there you have it. An array of whopping blunders crammed into a few sentences. StoneAge are comparing themselves, across the board, to another firm. They have failed to take responsibility for their profit fall and believe a generic solution will be the answer to their unique problems. They have not analysed their own business to see where the real problems lie. They will therefore continue their basic operations unchanged whilst expecting results to improve.

This is not uncommon. Companies regularly hide behind the latest buzz words, phrases and management guru prophecies as a substitute for an understanding of their own organisation. It reeks of a lack of thought, lack of initiative and lack of competence and of a copy-cat mentality. A few examples of my own to illustrate. A UK steel melter initiated a TQM program in an attempt to boost profits while still holding onto scientific management (rod of iron and ruling 'mafia') principals. Openness and mutual co-operation in a strict regime – there's a contradiction in there somewhere! Needless to say, it failed. A chemical company made the logistics department the centre of its operations because one of its rivals had done the same (and failed, incidentally). It was eventually disbanded. A steel distributor copied (literally) the productivity measures from a large UK engineering firm – two totally unrelated disciplines – and so produced meaningless figures and no better management control or understanding of its operations.

Issues like this may help you in future to glean valuable insights as to the future prosperity of your host organisation and so plan your next move before it is forced upon you.

But more directly relevant here is the illustration of the problem with prescriptive solutions. Taking the principals of these philosophies is fine, but you must adapt them to your own situation. And that is why, returning to the original principal behind this chapter, you will not find 'avenues to pursue' listed here. Instead, you will find ideas, suggestions, principals, techniques and food for thought, which you must then work on and apply to your individual circumstances. That way, you generate a bespoke solution for your own prosperity that you fully understand and believe in and which you can implement in a changing environment. This is your competitive advantage in today's corporate climate. This is the basis for developing your own self-managed career path, free from corporate rhetoric and reliance on out-dated company training programmes.

Let's add one or two more realities while we're at it. If you haven't yet been through some sort of redundancy program – either as a victim or as a survivor – you've either not been very around long, you've been living on Pluto or you should capitalise on your luck and start doing the lottery.

It's so easy to blame all sorts of factors for these 'forced' changes: economics, government policy, legislation, unions (or lack of), foreign investment, globalisation, currency fluctuations, cheap imports, etc., etc. I mean, when did you ever hear a UK manager say, "Sorry guys, we screwed up!", let alone something that requires proper thought like, "Yes, we failed to internationalise our operations quickly enough, despite knowing for years about the risks of a strong pound and Euro-scepticism. We didn't even have a contingency plan! So we've busted the chief executive down to laundryman." Some other event is always blamed.

If you've been a victim, chances are you'll work harder next time. Maybe you think you made mistakes or got on somebody's wrong side. You'll also probably feel an undercurrent of "My No.1 objective this time is to keep my bum firmly on this seat", or "Why should I flog myself? Didn't get me anywhere last time." Either way, you're unlikely to want to put yourself out much; more likely play it safe.

And if you were a survivor, the fall-out is one of low morale, de-motivation and distrust. Again, no basis for extra effort to progress. It seems to be a lose-lose situation for both employer and employee. In the next chapter, we'll look at how to gain capital from this apparent downwards spiral.

The fact is, the rate of change in business is accelerating. There are plenty of books on the matter if you would like to read further on this; I've included a couple of my preferred choices in the reading list. Keying into these new realities of employment requires a radically different approach towards career development and a radically different attitude to match. The supporting structure for this attitude we have discussed above in the five traits of a winner. There are far more than this, but these are central and critical. Depending on the type of person you are and your inherent personality traits, they may take some getting used to. They will, however, give you the confidence to tackle what follows. So before we stride out onto the recruitment racetrack, let's piece together a decent training program.

6

Capitalising On Chaos

The later chapters on interview techniques advocate that some of the most important qualities you can take to a prospective employer will not be on your CV. Your CV just gets you there, though it will also be good preparation for interview interrogation. However, an employer's final decision really rests on how you present yourself, what attitude you display, what personality you exude, how enthusiastic you appear and so on. These 'soft' elements of recruitment are become increasingly important to interviewers – part of the fall-out from a changed business environment.

As we have discussed already, the recessions of the 80's and 90's decimated the UK's primary manufacturing base and saw a sea-change in employment characteristics. Not only have jobs for life become extinct, temporary jobs have increased, worker protection has been stripped and simple job security is no more. In fact the UK is renowned for the ease in which employees can be laid off. This is one of the reasons why the UK attracts significant foreign investment. There never were any loyalties in business, but today, associations are ever more tenuous and fleeting.

On top of that, there is almost no area of an organisation that cannot be contracted out: secretarial, security, drivers, admin., payroll, IT, projects, engineering, maintenance, market research. Even organisational restructuring and business planning – the crux of middle to senior management occupation – can be bought from consultants. Come the revolution, any organisation will drop you faster than a maggoty apple, regardless of who you are.

So next time you listen to a personnel officer bang on about their fantastic development programmes, think how many people will be sticking around long enough to reap the benefits of such a programme in that same firm. This is often out-dated personnel departments desperately trying to justify their existence by clinging on to out-moded, prescribed practices, instead of adapting to the new order of things – or, rather, the new chaos – and redefining their role.

So where do we stand now? The result of all this de-layering, rationalisation and cost-cutting (aka firing people) is, for one, a 'flatter' organisational structure. The traditional hierarchical pyramid has all but disappeared. Instead, you have job-enrichment – a horizontal spread of responsibilities, blurring of demarcation lines, multi-skilling – and job-empowerment – a vertical integration of authority and delegation by management to lower grades. It all means that there is a greatly reduced chance of upwards promotion. Instead, you stay where you are and get dumped with more, possibly varied, work. And if there is promotion, it could be a big step.

Now to most people, this is disaster. It means they are going to be stuck in the same job, getting piled with more work, for the same pay, more stress and no prospects. Sound familiar? However, as always, there is a positive side. Let's see how.

1. Your expanded role means greater learning opportunities, a chance to broaden your skill base. That alone will add punch to your future CV, expand your options and possibilities and increase your marketability.

2. As a result, you have the chance to shift into a different role in a related field, or into a separate field altogether. For example, if you are currently a technical advisor for a firm which, as a cost-cutting measure, uses you, an office and IT as opposed to field-support, you may find that Sales aren't equipped with the depth of knowledge you have. You may find yourself out on the road with the sales person to discuss specifications before a supply agreement is drawn up. And there you have it: sales and marketing opportunities for you. If you're a maintenance engineer, who's been put in charge of his own budget, you may need to get trained in capital expenditure procedures and project management. To another firm, this may spell 'site engineer', 'field engineer' or 'project manager'.

3. You will gain a far broader network than you would otherwise have. You will then be in contact with people with knowledge of and contacts in a range of fields. We'll talk about networking on page 90.

4. Your extra responsibilities are just the opportunity you need to ply more training out of your employer. How can they refuse? You can

pick up all sorts of stuff you would never have the chance to learn in a more linear role.

5. With fewer people around, there is more responsibility for you to pick up on and people are generally paid according to the responsibility they carry. Dejected armies cry out for leaders. Be wary, though: the willing donkey carries the heaviest load. Make sure what you take on is important to you, that you keep records of your work and that you gain recognition for your initiatives at your next review. You will, of course, need to delegate some of your own workload. This is fine, because then you are in turn giving someone else the opportunity to expand themselves.

Whatever the organisation may think of your willingness, whatever rewards you may or may not get, your hidden agenda is to make yourself more marketable. Every new project, skill or competence strengthens your CV and makes you more attractive to other employers. Then you have more opportunity to search for what you want – more money, better prospects, a manager you respect, less stress, greater job satisfaction, more say in decisions, somewhere closer to home, less travel, more travel, and so on. Then you need not have to wait for an employer wanting something out of you before you get offered opportunities. With your options opening up, you no longer rely on a single employer for your development and advancement.

Now we're getting somewhere. Now, instead of being a corporate automaton, constantly under instruction and control, you are becoming a self-aware employee. The commercial factors that have altered the job market so radically are still relevant to your job security and duration of tenure at an employer, but now that you understand the realities of the market, these factors will not oppress you – you can see through them and exploit them. You are in control of your own career path and your positive approach enables you to make appropriate decisions in line with this. Never mind who or what's to blame. Never mind long-winded, boring analyses. The fact is, the market is highly fluid, which means you have to be highly adaptive. It's a fact of modern working. Organisations are geared up to quickly respond to rapidly changing market conditions. And so must you be. Here's a useful affirmation for you, related to Trait 5, above:

I Am Comfortable Being Uncomfortable.

73

"No chance", you may say. Perhaps rightly so. No one likes being uncomfortable. And all change is discomforting. If it wasn't, we'd have done it already. But this is a key trait to developing a winning attitude. Integrating thoughts like these into your action plans are vital in developing the resilience you're going to need to make it in today's employment arena. By taking a positive approach, as has been outlined here, it will not feel so discomforting, because you will be in charge of your own development. You have probably realised by now that the bottom line here is that you are essentially going it alone. And this is the subject of the next section.

"My Co."

So far, we have recognised that job security is no more and we have seen the need to take the initiative in career planning. We have covered some of the traits inherent to a winning attitude, identified how to extract capital from the new realities of employment and we have laid some of the foundations necessary for planning a self-managed career path. Following on from the five traits above, you will:

- Be taking an objective look at your own job, organisation and even business sector and gauging it against your own skills and qualifications, responsibilities, goals, desires and aspirations.

- Not be afraid to make decisions out of the ordinary, based on the incoherencies you have found between where you stand now and what you would like to be doing or where you believe you ought to be.

- Have realised that taking these decisions may involve some risk, but also that risk is necessary to progress.

- Have accepted total responsibility for your successes and mistakes.

- That you will be happy to pursue your plan because you know it is for your long-term benefit and will enable you to gain control over your own career, rather than relying on 'organisational benevolence' or the flow of the tide.

If you accept this for yourself, then "My Co." is about to go into business and it will go to the highest bidder. With that kind of '100% responsibility' attitude, you are no longer an expendable corporate asset or are vulnerable to the ebb and flow of the market, waiting for the next tide to sweep you away. You are a versatile, self-propelled vessel that can seek new ports, trade its wares, pick up new cargo and move on.

Well, after that dramatic revelation, let's take a small but important digression for a moment.

Everyone who knows how to sit on a chair knows that safety and security are the basic foundations upon which is built any 'hierarchy of needs', which goes something like this:

Higher needs   *Met through:*

Self-actualisation   The realisation of one's full potential through satisfying curiosity, learning, freedom to enquire and express, promotional opportunities, creativity, challenge.

Esteem   Achievement, confidence, recognition, reward, prestige, appreciation and respect of oneself.

Social   Sense of belonging, social activities, friendships, open communication.

Safety   Freedom from threat; security, predictability.

Physiological   Usually relates to basic elements of survival; here, we relate to agreeable physical working conditions and an acceptable salary.

Basic needs

There are variations on this, but this scale will serve our purposes nicely.

The basic needs have to be satisfied before the higher ones can be realised. If your very livelihood is in constant doubt, how can you focus on contributing to the collective effort? How can you focus your energies towards your own development when you are so pre-occupied with survival? How can you plan your future if your present is not even certain? The answer is, you can't. So how does an organisation develop winning teams and generate dedication from it's employees, if the 'team' is in a state of constant flux and the members are always looking over their shoulders? Answer: it doesn't. An enlightened firm will know this and will know how to benefit from an individual's need for self-development. If it rewards and develops such people, it will prosper. If it doesn't, it won't and they will move on, or vice versa. More to the point, how can you prosper if your typical organisation can't get these basics right?

Well, now that we are developing a view and an attitude coherent with the realities of today's market, we are getting into the right frame of mind to do some realistic career planning. We can now look at what you can do in practice to support and develop your winning attitude into a self-managed career path. What follows is necessarily brief. It would be impractical to have lengthy discussions about each of the elements mentioned below, as they are both inherently subjective, and so for your own analysis, and are potentially big topics in themselves.

So... give each one careful thought, then apply them to yourself to build upon the work you have already done. Tricky, I know – it's never easy being objective in such subjective matters. Because of this, when I mentioned earlier about making mistakes, this is where most of them will be made. Unless you already have a glorious widescreen, Technicolor, surround-sound vision of your own dreams and aspirations, which most of us don't, you will find it takes a while to get to "your truth" – and you probably wouldn't be reading this book anyway!

You may find you make judgements based on what you currently do. All other possibilities and options are not considered or are regarded as too obscure, distant, impractical, uncertain, impossible even. You think you know which way to go because it sits nicely with your present situation, with your present thoughts, abilities and, most of all, your current *perceived* restrictions. Despite *knowing* that you should be thinking outside the box, it may take a while and a few trial and error cycles to realise you are still restraining your imagination and stifling your options. Remember my own story about being in manufacturing?

However, the following points will help a great deal. Again, they will require some work on your part, as some are highly introspective exercises, but all are very valuable ones.

A Five-Point Plan For "My Co."

There are five inter-related elements you'll need to address to develop your resilience to the vagaries of the job market and to market your own My Co. They are:
- Potential
- Learning ability
- Willingness to develop
- Self-confidence
- Self-esteem

Let's look at each of them in turn and see how they all piece together.

(i) Potential.

You can't move on without it. Potential means you have some sort of untapped resources. What sort of potential, you will have to figure out. Where did Einstein's potential lie? As a clerk? OK, you can't get much more radical than that, but the principal is one of realisation and then of having the commitment to assert yourself to your cause.

Alternatively, and more commonly, you could apply your skill(s) to a different area. An Olympic sprinter called Renaldo Nehemiah used his speed to make millions in Pro GridIron football as a wide receiver. These are the human whippets that hurtle down the wings almost faster than the poor quarterback can hurl the pigskin.

You see the principal. Now let's turn it to more usual situations. Would you rather be a fitter or an installation engineer, travelling across Europe, all expenses paid? Both use mechanical and/or electrical knowledge. Would you rather be an operations manager or a productivity consultant? Both understand management systems, performance indicators, plant layout and the like. Would you rather be a receptionist or a tour guide? Both are clear, pleasant speakers, organised, approachable and communicative. It's your choice. In all cases, you apply your core competencies to broaden your scope, to increase your knowledge and your abilities, often for greater purpose, greater personal gain or greater job satisfaction.

A Word About Skills

And that word is "transferable". To broaden your options in this manner, you first of all need to identify your skills. Skills are things you carry out in practice. It may help to identify them by thinking in terms of '-ing' words (administering, treating, writing, maintaining, advising, designing, evaluating, examining, devising, computing, coaching, negotiating, etc.). You will find these skills are common to a number of different careers.

Our engineer above may be versed in maintaining machinery, assessing safety issues, designing plant layout, dismantling and re-building machines and so on. The manager may describe himself as adept at constructing control systems, analysing data or process flows, communicating intentions, selling or presenting ideas, identifying and solving problems. The receptionist may be good at communicating, advising, arranging itineraries, organising events (meetings, conferences) and so on. You can see how these skills can be directly related to the alternative careers suggested for each. Whatever roles you can uncover where you could equally apply your own '-ing' words, you stand as good a chance of success in these roles as you do in your present position, albeit with a little extra application, perhaps.

Now back to the plot. To recognise your skills is to draw on your abilities. You have recognised what you're good at – and what you're not so good at – and that you have the potential to build on those skills and enhance your accomplishments so far. Muddling through in your current position is fine, but when you move on, you really ought to be focusing on your strengths. No one can do everything, but everyone can do something. Find or decide on your something and go out and do it.

Whatever you do, don't wait for seven swans to fly over your house, for the stars to align, for your horoscope to say it's OK, or for your destiny to fall out of a fortune cookie. The decision is yours and yours alone. Fire your imagination. My grandfather used to say: "It's not a matter of doing what you like, it's liking what you do." That may have been OK for someone living their formative years in a depression, where any job was a blessing, but it will hardly do today. These days, it smacks of a defeatist attitude, of accepting and restricting yourself to your 'lot', however meagre or stifling. I'm not saying that you will ever find a panacea where everything in the garden is always rosy. But there's a big world full of infinite variety out there. Nothing is perfect, but with a modicum of commitment and effort, you can have a real good go at finding what suits you.

A quick example. I used to work with a chappie who had always wanted to be an airline pilot. Quite literally – always; for as long as he can remember. How many of us can boast of even having a *real* childhood dream? He had the ability and the commitment, yet there he was, in his mid-thirties, frustrating himself every day by trawling all over Europe selling somebody else's wares. And when he could be so much happier ...and richer! This guy had everything he needed to get his ideal job. And still he languished. He was certainly going to do it one day, but how many times have we heard that one before?

Incidentally, he also had a flair for languages (Dutch, German, French and Italian at last count, I think). He was also one of life's unflappables, describing hair-raising incidents on snow-covered autobahns as 'interesting' from a technical and driving-skill point of view! An obscure quality, you may think, but a vital one I would wager for a pilot. You may be similarly surprised to find where some of your own 'softer' talents may lie.

(ii) Learning ability.

OK, so you've recognised your talents and your potential, now you need to capitalise on it by showing yourself just what you can learn. That's why I mentioned before about knowing your strengths. My pilot friend used to work silly hours and still find the time and energy to do his studies – I saw them; they were mind-blowing! Planes also fascinated him. He enjoyed it. Do you think if that wasn't true, he would ever find the time? As you learn new aptitudes, you too will need to find the time from somewhere, which will often mean sacrifices in other areas at first. If you don't have a certain flair for what you do or get a bit of a kick out of it, do you also think you're going to stick with it long enough to make it count?

Now a great many of you will say, "Work is not fun. Who actually *likes* going to work?" A good point. It first of all depends on the nature of the work. Refer back to your skills, strengths and development traits for an answer to that one. It will be more enjoyable if you are engaged in something you are good at and if you have a desire to improve in that field. Then you will be willing and able to strive for that improvement. Secondly, it depends on what's called the 'psychological contract'. This needs a bit of explanation.

79

People seek fulfilment of certain elements of their hierarchy of needs (mentioned previously) from different areas of their life. Some people actually view job security as low priority because they are already on a self-managed career path or they want to broaden their experience in their field. They voluntarily move from job to job seeking their best reward, whether it be more money, autonomy, the permission to try new ideas, or whatever. For others, security is everything. Perhaps they have a young family or are approaching retirement. If what you get from your employer is not in tune with your requirements, the psychological contract is not fulfilled. You are unhappy, dis-satisfied and demotivated. Ask yourself what you seek in your job.

You may liken it to a personal relationship. Your essential "lad", for example, is probably not too bothered about "relationships" in the traditional sense, a mortgage or the biological clock. Anybody who ends up with such a social butterfly would rightly feel distrust, insecurity and uncertainty about the future. You essentially have three options in life: live with it, change it or leave it. Let's say in this case, the only option is to leave; any other avenue would be stressful, futile and a waste of energy and attention. Similarly, let's say you need security and flexible hours in your job and are willing to settle for a reasonable, though perhaps uninspiring, wage to find them. You will need to be in an organisation which is not on the ropes, has good employee protection policies and which has a more open approach to working hours. If this doesn't sound like your employer, then you have a similar choice to make. You will never find your required peace of mind without those policies.

It should be noted here that firms do need both types of employee. They need the 'sticker', the 'not-going-anywhere-thank-you-very-much' person as resident experts. And experts they must be – able to hold the fort, to know the work and the systems inside out, to train newcomers who seek to learn and then move on. This latter type is also critical. Without them, how would the business ever develop?

Those that seek *all* of their satisfactions from the one job, however, are in trouble. You can not take the risks of growth and expect absolute security as well. Dedication, by all means. Dependency? No thanks. For those who do seek to grow, another, extremely valuable affirmation to help get things in perspective:

High Commitment; Low Attachment

If you think about it, this is actually a good way of summing up your "My Co." attitude: committed to your current position, as you are learning and growing, but it is of little consequence if you need to or choose to move on. If dis-satisfactions creep in, you are willing and able to take the calculated risk of playing the market to improve your lot. Once you have that, you can forge ahead with your third element.

(iii) Willingness to develop.

To develop yourself, you must be willing to step out of your comfort zone, be willing to take on new ideas, concepts, projects, skills and challenges. Sacrifices may be necessary and a certain amount of risk required to see your efforts come to fruition. Not only does it take some will power to take the step in the first place, but you may need to spread yourself a little thinner for a while, re-adjust your priorities or change your itineraries. Sustaining through these changes often requires greater will than starting in the first place.

Crucial to maintaining your will is the desire to succeed. This desire should precipitate from the plans you make for yourself. Once you have realised what it takes to develop your own self-managed career path and where your initiatives can take you, you will have formulated an image or an idea of how you would like your career to develop. This is your future self. Compare that with your current self and you see the gap. A gap that can only be filled by action. The desire to fill that gap is what drives you to action. If the picture of your future self is not what you really want, you will not feel the same desire to fill the gap, you won't be able to get excited about the work and the prospects in front of you, you will not act with commitment and your plans will fade. This means it is time to re-think, re-assess and re-analyse. A little reflection now can save an awful lot of disappointment later on.

If you thought it was hard to generate the will first time round, wait until you try for the second or third time. At this point, you may feel like you are going in circles. On the plus side (as always), as you try a few options that don't work, you narrow your parameters and so gain accuracy in your future decisions. Your confidence should, ironically, grow.

(iv) Self-confidence.

Continuing the above point, when you come to determine your points of action, you will need the confidence and the ability to "see outside the box", to stand clear of the masses and of your own, often self-imposed, restrictions and to venture forth from your safe little rut. The clearer your image about your future development, the greater will be your confidence to work towards it. Projecting this confidence may take time, especially if you have suffered before at the hands of corporate blunders or by your own decisions.

Earlier, I mentioned about growing in small, incremental steps, not great leaps and bounds. This is important here. In time, you can look back and see how much your career has progressed, but day to day or week to week, take it an inch at a time. Each time you put another step forward and find firm ground, you will grow a little in confidence. Take a flying leap into the unknown and heaven knows where you will land. That's not being in control. Those grains of confidence will eventually coalesce into firmer ground and you will feel better about taking bigger steps. Then your pace quickens and you begin to grow exponentially. Try to do too much too soon and you may flounder and waste a great deal of energy in simply recovering from the knocks.

Whenever you decide to take on new responsibilities, a new challenge or new ideas, a certain apprehension is inevitable. So, here's another useful affirmation – this time to help turn this natural apprehension into anticipation:

You Don't Know You've Been In Prison Until You Break Out.

This brings us onto our fifth point.

(v) Self-esteem.

Let's assume now that you are breaking new ground and entering what may be for you uncharted territory, involving full career responsibility and a self-managed career path. To forge ahead down this path, you will firmly need to believe that you are doing the right thing, that you are eminently capable of seeing this through and of surviving in a fluid market. You need to be comfortable with taking charge of your own development, your own success and the rate of your own advancement and of coping with the risks and the setbacks. This, of course, is self-esteem.

Another one for the self-improvement gurus, self-esteem is basically an inner belief that you have value and that you are capable of realising that value. Self-esteem brings conviction, backed by the confidence to see your convictions through. It gives you the inner strength and the will to step outside your comfort zone and evolve.

Let's just be clear about one thing, though. Self-esteem does not include extroversion, arrogance, conceit or aggressive behaviours. You can have all these things and still be left empty when you get fired or when your spouse gives you a slating. In fact you'll probably go into pure retaliation mode to try and 'assert your authority'.

True self-esteem will elevate you above this because you know your inner values. You can recognise and acknowledge your short-comings, agree with criticism or discard it as mis-guided or mis-informed. If you get rejected at interview, you will know you either need to hone your techniques, or they have failed to recognise your strengths, abilities and potential because they do not themselves fully understand what they seek. In which case, a better opportunity awaits you within a more enlightened organisation. Either way, it is not a personal setback; it is another valuable insight into where and how you might move forward.

Thus far, we have principally considered the personal, softer, self-development aspects of job hunting. We began by looking at how the job market has changed as a result of corporate re-structuring and the fluidity of the market and at the need to free yourself from dependency on any one organisation for your career development – a direct response to the speed of change in modern business. We considered the emergence of knowledge as the primary driver of productivity. We have listed some of the more important traits you need to develop to maintain a winning attitude for your survival and prosperity in these turbulent times. We have discussed how you can extract the positive from this new reality. And we have charted a five-point action plan to gear yourself up for a self-managed career path, one that will allow you to gain capital from this apparent chaos.

We covered this first because it takes thought, it takes application and it takes practice. If you approach job hunting as simply a matter of learning how to write letters in response to advertisements, you're playing a mug's game. Like people who squander the rent money on horses because it looks like a "dead cert" in the paper, you are operating without rhyme or reason or understanding of the game you are playing. It's just the next hopeful punt. You should by now be getting a firmer grasp of the *nature* of the game (for there are no strict rules) and be starting to see how you can find your most favourable odds.

The material covered so far is a longer-term strategy, not an overnight fix to a snap decision. You need to start now. You may be in for a lot of mistakes, re-thinks and adjustments. But remember, even though you may err from time to time, never second-guess yourself. When you act on a decision, you must act without self-doubt. That is a true test of self-confidence and conviction. You are always acting in your best interests and using the best knowledge you have at the time. Hindsight is great, but you don't have that yet. And if you vacillate in indecision, you'll get nowhere. Maintain your convictions. That's confidence. Accept your mistakes, learn from them and believe you will triumph. That's self-esteem. Accept 100% responsibility for your own direction and career path, it's set-backs and successes. Maintain a high commitment to your cause, but with low attachment, should circumstances change and require you to adjust. That's the winning attitude. Now let's put it to the test.

7

Into The Fray

Just about everything on the newsagent's shelf has job ads in it these days. Well, at least the ones within easy reach all seem to. Now we also have the Internet to contend with. With unemployment (apparently) falling and skill shortages rising, you'd think you'd have loads of choice and it would be a cinch to dig up a decent job. Unfortunately, this situation also means that companies are having to compete a little to attract good people, which makes jumping ship attractive to those already in work. On average, you will probably have to contend with more people looking to move jobs than you will those currently unemployed. So it never really gets any easier – unless you happen to be a graduate, who have their own particular territory to fight over.

The following sections give an assessment of the typical channels you can investigate to track down your job. At the risk of stating the obvious, now that you are "My Co." and not someone else's corporate asset, it makes sense to have job-hunting as part of your 'business plan'. Keep you options open, keep an eye on the market, maintain your intelligence network and keep your finger on the pulse. Quite possibly, you'll know that the time is right to move way before you gain the conviction to take action. You will need to nurture the confidence to take action when your instincts tell you to. Move around too much though, and you'll look like a fly-by-night.

National Newspapers

Let's get this one out of the way first – don't bother! These are out of the league of most people and often handled by recruitment agencies, so if you're on their books and you're suitable, they'll call you…maybe.

Even so, imagine the response rate. You'll also be lucky to find local vacancies (unless you live in London), by which I mean within forty minutes of your home. You'd have to be on big money or desperate to justify, say, two hours of your day just to get there.

Occasionally you will find an intriguing one in the small ads at the end (the column-inch type). They are necessarily short, so you'll usually need to call to get more info. This is good, because you can glean enough from a five-minute conversation to decide whether you want to apply or not. List a few questions before you call. Your CV and job objective will help you cut to the chase. Worth more of your time than the big ads, anyway.

Job Centres

Another one to dismiss before we start looking properly. Very localised, very poor selection. There used to be an executive register, but that got binned. If you desperately want to be a delivery driver or work all hours in a shop, then by all means... Next, please!

Local Newspapers

Unless you're in a specialised field, these are your best bet of any publication. The down side is that this is also the first point of call for most people. Rather than get your town or city daily paper, you may find (if you live within striking distance of a conurbation) an all-encompassing weekly, imaginatively titled after the region it covers ("Jobs North-West" for example). These collect all the ads from all the regional dailies and lump them together for your enjoyment.

The principal problems associated with this avenue of pursuit revolve around CVs, the large quantity an advert typically attracts and their general quality (or lack of). This automatically makes the recipient want to sift out 90-odd percent of them very quickly indeed. That is why these ads generally get the thumbs down in job-search books. Not, I believe, because you've got no chance of success *per se*, but because you've got no chance of success with the typical standard of CV that people produce. With so many to sift through, it makes the recruiter's job a daunting one. You try excavating the important bits from several dozen two-page 'autobiographies' and see if you can keep *your* head off the desk. No wonder otherwise good candidates get missed. That's what can make it a bit of a lottery.

Reading between the lines, though, if you get yourself a good CV (which you have!), you'll stand head and shoulders above the rest and drastically increase your chances of getting a reasonable job locally.

Specialist fields, such as teaching, civil service and the medical profession also have their own publications, available in most libraries. Local government ones are sometimes in a separate file.

You'll notice how some ads, particularly in the nationals, which is another reason to avoid them, almost ask for the Archangel Gabriel to apply. You know the sort: mid-twenties, degree, two languages, five years at middle management level, 20k. Yeah, right! For a start, if you've got a degree, you'll only have been working two or three years anyway. This interprets as "Blue chip company, or self-important manager of a middling firm, wants rare, top-grade, university high-flyer with unparalleled ability and enthusiasm to work all hours God sends for the kind of wage they can get in three months elsewhere." I'm exaggerating, obviously, but they do crop up.

This type of advert you might see again a few weeks later when they've got their heads on straight. This time it may read: "Graduate calibre, experience of supervision in an office environment, influencing skills, a second language would be useful." Now you can read this as, "If you've been to college and have some youthful fire, we've got a bunch of uncoordinated, idle donkeys in our sales department we'd like you to sort out."

You'll need to watch the classifieds carefully to spot these. You can then write in and say something like, "I see you've not found your ideal person yet. Well, I can do (this, that and the other) and, although I have only two years' supervisory experience, it *has* been in a high-pressure environment and I would love to improve on my school languages, for which I got an A-grade." Or some such.

In reality, a perfect candidate is never really found. This kind of response will get you close and you can fill in the gap by coming across as particularly enthusiastic – and, of course, with your killer CV!

A quick aside here. Notice how, in the reply, I sandwiched the negative (less experience than required) between two positives. It's a common tactic: you don't want to start or end your argument on a bum note, so you slot it in the middle.

Another drawback with newspaper ads is that a good portion of employers simply don't use them – or so the surveys suggest. So let's look at some other avenues.

Agencies

It costs you nothing except a few stamps and phone calls, so get with as many as possible, particularly if you're unemployed or if time is not on your side. Then you will have particular need to cover all the angles and will feel better leaving no stone unturned. You may never visit most of the agencies you write to, but you can bet your boots the one you don't approach will have the job that's right for you. As it costs you next to nothing, what have you got to lose? Occasionally you will get invited in so they can fill out their own application forms or database records. Often, though, you will only be invited if they have a vacancy for you, so don't get too disappointed if you hear nothing. Despite what people say, calling in from time to time pays no dividends. If they are half good at their job, you won't have to. And if everyone did it, they'd do little else but answer empty enquiries.

There are definite pros and cons to using these people. On the one hand, they do have access to large numbers of vacancies, some of which may not even be advertised or may be out of your area and so you would not otherwise get to know about.

A good portion of agency ads, though, you will still find in the newspapers. That's because some poor soul spends the vast part of their day cold-calling the same advertisers you see to ask if they want to use their services and to tell them they have hundreds of clients on their books, all of indisputable quality and they are sure they will have someone to match their profile – for 10% of their first year's salary, naturally. This wonderful task usually falls to the new kid on the block who needs to build his own client base. He's easy to spot. He's the one with the local paper spread across his desk, absently running his biro back and forth through the last ad that turned him down, as he recites his spiel into the phone for the benefit of his next prospect. Sometimes you see at the bottom of an ad 'no agencies, please'. That's why.

On the other hand, it adds an extra layer to the people you have to deal with and sell yourself to. Agency staff are often sales people themselves, so they do at least know how to execute the appropriate process to satisfy demand. I say "should", because I have found there is a broad spectrum of quality with recruitment agencies. Out of the hundreds I have contacted, I found only a handful worth bothering with and they were not necessarily the biggest, either. There are reasons for this.

There are likely to be only a few in your area who are capable of dealing with your particular situation and needs. Many, though, will take your CV because it costs them nothing and maybe because it then allows them to say they have huge numbers of clients. I understand that some of the larger agencies attract so many CVs that they scan them into a computer, or have you fill out their own forms which someone then types in. They are then filtered using key word recognition to extract candidates. So if you failed to use the correct words on your CV to describe yourself, you're scuppered. It can also lead to some gross misunderstandings. I have been sent to wholly inadequate vacancies, even to the point where the employer said (and I quote), "I really can't understand why you're here", and often been telephoned to discuss similarly unsuitable, below par or unrelated posts.

There are specialist agencies for IT, law, accountancy, sales, media, construction and probably some others, but don't ignore the one-person operation either. They are typically long-time servants of their field (chemists, metallurgists, electronics engineers, etc.), who now specialise in matching people with their contacts in the industry. You are more likely to find them in the respective trade journals than in the phone books. It will not be clear in the latter exactly what they do.

For the rest of us, the medium firms seem to offer the better service. Here you get more individual attention and the small number of people there have good scope for growth and so the chance of big bonuses.

I would advise you to call any agency first. Not only to make sure they operate in your field, but also so you can start your letter with: "As requested, I have enclosed my CV". Then you are more likely to get a proper reading. No doubt they get dozens every day and might find it a presumptuous addition to the tedium to have to rake through yet another pile of speculative CVs. If you enquire first, you can save time, effort and money and direct your letter to the correct person by name.

Many agency people are massively busy. If you don't cut the mustard with them, you won't get an invite to the party. You have to be quick, concise and positive, which is good practice, really. They typically deal with the 'harder' side of recruitment, filtering appropriately qualified candidates before passing them on to the client organisation. So, if you've done your homework on your CV, you will find this experience considerably easier.

If you don't land a job first time around with an agency, you are unlikely to get a second call. Not unless the feedback is that you clearly did well throughout the process and it was a close call. No doubt they have their reasons: change of personnel (staff turnover is sometimes quite alarming), so a new database of clients gets built up, bad feedback from the employer, a million other people to test...

Occasionally, you will get calls from agencies perhaps a year after you first spoke. This is either the database key-word filter at work or a competent staff member managing his own database well. With some databases, until someone clears it out or they have an updating procedure, your name will continue to be spat out on occasion. I consider this a lazy and inaccurate way of conducting what is a critical operation for both you and the employer...but that's the way of the world.

The Internet

If you've never seen the Internet, you've been living in a cave. If you're not familiar with computers, you need to go back to school before you go job hunting. Some people will boast they don't need to know about "those bloody things", but these days, that's a dangerous blind spot in anyone's knowledge.

If you don't know how to use the Internet, I suggest you familiarise yourself. BBC TV still advertises free introduction courses at colleges throughout the country. If you don't have your own PC, you will probably have a friend that does. Pay the phone bill you incur and they are unlikely to object. If they do, they're not much of a mate! Failing that, there's always the library, where the staff are only too keen to help. They do charge by the hour and you will probably have to book.

Like any other Internet subject, there are dozens of sites to choose from. Some are easier to use than others. Some categorise vacancies by region (north-west, south-east, Wales or whatever), rather than by town. Some allow very specific search criteria to be entered, which permits you to sift through thousands of vacancies in a matter of seconds – quicker even than going through your local paper.

There is talk that the Internet process fails to deliver. As it is still in its infancy, it would be inappropriate to judge it too harshly yet. It is, however, likely to continue growing, as advertising here is many times cheaper than in the papers, even the local ones. Suck it and see.

Networking

I must confess I hate this word. It has a very eighties 'must do lunch' feel, or an old-boy, closed-shop ring about it. Unfortunately that's how many people perceive it, too. Networking is assumed to mean capitalising on insider contacts for favours and preferential treatment, or getting a free 'leg-up' the corporate ladder. That definition smacks of gang-like behaviour, capable of lasting damage to an organisation and ruining an individual's credibility through unjustifiably and corruptly providing a wholly unsuitable position. All for the sake of a quick power trip.

Real networking is the process of forming and using contacts and associations, either personal, professional or social, to interrogate the potential job market. It's a longer-term process that requires consummate

90

professionalism. It is often a preferred method for employers as it reduces both the costs of recruitment and the risks associated with traditional methods. Bearing in mind that there is a strong element of trust in recruiting through a network contact, so you must be open and honest about your intentions and motives.

Working through personal and social contacts is simple enough. Professional contacts require a certain informal etiquette. If you're pursuing a new line, for example, ask to be introduced by someone who already knows this person. Alternatively, write a letter of introduction saying from whom you got the lead and that you will call, say, next week. Chapter 4 includes a couple of examples. Remember, although it may turn out to be mutually beneficial in the end, you are at first using *their* valuable time for *your* purposes.

If you meet up, make it informal but purposeful. You can also get hints from your new contact if they are aware of other possible opportunities, aspiring firms or areas of interest. And always thank them afterwards. You could also offer to reciprocate the network intelligence for their benefit, to help keep them keen.

Of course, some people are naturally adept at cultivating large circles of acquaintances; others not. You just need to be bold enough to ask. As stated, the end result needs to be mutually beneficial, so you may be doing someone else a favour by openly marketing yourself. Looking at it that way makes it easier to present yourself.

Do keep a log of all your contacts and of the dates you were in touch. File all your letters and keep notes of important points from conversations and the like. You will then always be up to speed on where you stand and, most importantly, never miss a potential lead.

Advert Jargon

If you read some job ads, you will find little more than a collection of popular phrases and buzz words strung together into pretty sentences, which can be interpreted in a number of ways, or which leave you with no real picture of what the job entails. Your own job description may be a good example! Often you have to read between the lines. People often read ads with the same lack of attention with which they were written.

Below are some of the more common phrases in ad-jargon. Don't take them too literally or seriously; some are the product of pure cynicism – or protectionism, depending upon your viewpoint. Be advised, though, some ads do a pretty good Cheshire Cat impression – all smiles and no substance!

Advert jargon deciphered...

Unspecified salary: £Competitive/ an excellent salary for the right person/ commensurate with age and experience/ no mention at all.

If it was worth shouting about they would, then they would certainly attract top applicants. Usually translates as "low salary". Also, age is discriminatory and if you haven't got the experience, you won't be accepted – so why mention it?

Phrases like "up to £x", "our best sales people earn £y" and so on should be ignored.

One guy may have earnt the stated amount in one week when he got lucky, but never again. You're likely to be worked to death.

Self-starter.

"You're on your own, probably on commission. Expect lots of ass-kicking at the slightest provocation, but not much in the way of real support."

Communication skills.

"You won't be working on your own, but everyone else uses this phrase and we're not sure how else to describe it." You should be able to work it out from the job title and chief responsibilities. e.g. for a marketing assistant, presentations will feature; for a sales co-ordinator, telephone manner and structuring a conversation are key; for a shift manager, you'll be holding meetings, making out reports, maybe run inter-department projects. If you want a good laugh, ask!

Management trainee.

"Manager's gopher", or, "You'll be starting at the bottom like everyone else."

Organisational skills.	"There's lots of paperwork" or, "We've not much formal control over what happens here, you'll need your wits about you and we want you to stop our workforce running rings round us."
Work under pressure.	We're disorganised and spend much of our time fire-fighting, because we have inadequate management controls and/or too few people.
Take your next career move in this forward-thinking company.	"Have more of the same. We want your experience without having to train you."
Fast expanding company.	Networking schemes.

One final, important point to make. Cut out every advert you apply to, or copy it all down for future reference and make a note of the following:
- The day you sent it.
- To whom you sent it and their job title.
- The reply.
- Any interview dates.
- Rejections.

It's a terrible feeling not knowing where all your applications stand. It's also reassuring to look at your record sheet and see that you still have some outstanding. There are psychological benefits, too. You may have one most promising application lined up. As you attend others, you may look upon them as secondary, as practice for 'the biggie'. That takes an enormous amount of pressure off. As a result, you may well surprise yourself and put in an admirable performance and wind up in the enviable position of having more than one offer to consider. Stranger things have happened at sea. If nothing else, you can at least see that everything doesn't rest on just one remaining application – now that's pressure we can all do without.

Closing Comment

It is often said that the majority of vacancies are filled through networking. It would be folly, however, to rely on any one channel. If you are out of work, then job hunting is your full-time occupation. You will be scanning every newspaper and journal, telephoning every agent in the business and talking to everyone you know. You will be rifling the business news to see who is doing well and who isn't – you don't want to miss a clue, a hint or the one piece of information that could make all the difference.

If you are in work, I would recommend you develop an intelligence-gathering routine. Whether you are considering jumping ship or not, it pays to keep your feelers out – who knows what machinations are going on in the boardroom? If you're in no immediate hurry, you can wait for that great job to turn up, but you wouldn't want to miss it. Scan the Net once a week, pop into the library Saturday morning and keep your list on contacts up to date and on the boil. This is, after all, your livelihood. Protect it and nurture it.

You have now covered the difficult part. The next stage, however, is more intense because it brings all your efforts thus far into sharp focus. When you get to the interview stage, you will need to give it your undivided attention and let it be the single focus of your days. You may even need to let your current work take a back seat. It will, after all, soon be history. If you just take the odd morning off to attend, you're jeopardising a lot of hard work, tough training and a glittering future for the sake of inadequate preparation, apathy or over-confidence. So stay focused and be ready to shift up a gear.

8

Preparing For Interview

I failed the second year of my degree through sheer boredom and disillusionment. Then a friend imparted to me some real education. He first of all explained the fact that the degree was just a means to an end. The objective was a well-paid job – money. The specialised knowledge was just incidental. Second, to realise that objective, he gave me an exam strategy and it went like this.

First, research your exam history. Get hold of as many past papers as possible and draw a matrix of question subjects against the years they appear. That will tell you which ones are core questions and crop up every year and which ones are optionals and alternate years. He was right, there was a clear pattern in around 80% of subjects.

Secondly, out of say 8 subjects, there would be only four questions. So pick the four most obvious from the matrix (five for safety, if revision time permitted) and do a really thorough job on those. Go to the library and, one subject after the other, get all the relevant books out and construct a huge essay. Then condense it into a manageable length, making sure it flows so that it's easier to remember.

When it's finished, re-write the essay over and over again to memorise it; not word-for-word, but do include all relevant facts. Then finally, make a list of the first word from each paragraph, take the first letter from each of these words and write them in order. Perhaps create a little rhyme to aid memory. When the question appears in the exam, remember the rhyme, write down the letters, expand into words and let the essay flow out.

"Do that," he said, "and you'll romp it." I did. I doubled my percentages with only half the workload.

And the moral of the story? Information and preparation are two of the most powerful weapons you possess. This philosophy is a central feature of this book and particularly so in the following chapters. When you know what's coming and you have prepared for it, your confidence soars, your abilities multiply and your success rate dramatically increases. This approach completely undermines the opposition's power-base, a point I will re-emphasise in chapter 9.

Right. Business. Chapters 5 to 7 focused on adopting a winning attitude towards today's fluid and unpredictable job market. They advocated developing certain winning traits, to objectively analyse your own situation, abilities, goals and objectives. And they outlined how to adopt a positive approach to potentially demoralising situations, all with the explicit aim of developing your own self-managed career path, free from corporate rhetoric and the vagaries of the job market and detached from reliance on out-dated company training programmes. This requires a degree of subjectivity and so could not be overtly described within the confines of an agenda, a series of instructions or a to-do list.

The interview process is different. It is riddled with rules of engagement, standard practices and etiquette. This allows a more instructional format for these chapters. Do keep in mind, though, that careers, business sectors, employers and employees are all variables. Any combination of which can vary the ingredients for success in the interview process. A generalist approach is therefore necessary. Nevertheless, most of what you will find here can be applied to the majority of interview situations.

If you have followed chapters 2 to 4, your CV will include only directly job-relevant information and does not waste valuable space on 'personal stuff'. If interviewers want to know about your hobbies, marital status, age and health, they will ask at interview. Pre-judging you on such issues is either irrelevant or discriminatory, so we don't give them the opportunity to do so.

The job of your CV is, first and foremost, to get you into interview. In preparing the information for your CV you are, as a by-product, developing good, concise, specific answers to guaranteed interview questions. So let's take it as read that your résumé has done its job and got you in the door. How do you then give yourself the best chance of living up to the high expectation they will now have of you and of ultimately winning through? This is what the rest of this book is all about.

Largely, the old, formalised methods of 'text book' recruitment are disappearing. Larger firms may have the money and resources to go through the long process of determining candidate criteria from a defined job profile and may still believe in a detailed, structured process of assessing each candidate against those criteria. But the number of large firms is falling. In addition, with job descriptions becoming broader and demarcation lines more diffuse, this is becoming less of an exact science and the softer side of appropriate candidacy is becoming increasingly important. In other words, do you have the people skills? Do they like your style? And do they like you?

And when you consider you are up against others of similar qualification and experience levels as you, that makes creating the right personal impression pretty much critical.

So we will first cover necessary preparation and important elements, particularly related to presentation, that you may need to practice beforehand, so that they become more natural by the time you are on show. You'll be given an overview of the types of interview you can expect and the pros and cons of each, to help you stay objective about them and not be intimidated. Then we will look at actual interview questions and some useful answers to each. There will be some tips on what to say and what not to say and also some questions you can ask in return. Finally, there is advice on what to do after the event and on issues to consider before accepting an offer.

As always, preparation is everything. Your only concern during an interview should be your answers. But there are so many other aspects that go into the mix, you really ought to practice as much as possible before you go.

Even so, before you say a word in an interview, they will first clap eyes on you. Subconsciously, books *are* judged by their cover; people don't feel comfortable until they can pigeon-hole you into one of their recognised image categories. If you look successful, you'll be perceived as successful. So let's do personal image some justice and look at it first, to see if you need to go shopping.

<u>Clothing and General Appearance</u>

You only get one chance to make a first impression. It's a piece of wisdom that has been so over-used it has become a cliché, and like all clichés, it has lost most of its original impact.

People look at you in the following order: tie (if you have one), then hair, then shoes. In that order. If ladies wear a striking lapel brooch, bright buttons or neckerchief, these are most likely to draw first attention ...then hair, then shoes. Actually, you should try to avoid anything too striking, such as excessive jewellery, prominent accessories and very bright colours; it'll just put the interviewer off. Oh, and go easy on the perfume.

Men should wear a silk tie – and not one with Bugs Bunny or South Park on it. Subtly colourful is OK, as long as it's not too gaudy and looks like it should come with it's own volume control! Tie pins are OK, but don't sit too well on plain, dark ties. And for goodness sake, don't wear white socks. Make sure your suit is clean and pressed. Darker suits are better. Dark blue best of all. Massive wrinkles in the trousers and the back of your jacket look awful, so avoid cloths susceptible to this. Ideally, your trouser legs should not show your socks when you walk. Get in front of a full-length mirror and take a normal step forward. If your socks peek out, your trousers are a little short. Conversely, make sure they don't trail on the floor either!

Overall, and going by the adage that a bank will only offer you a loan if you don't need one, you should aim to look like you don't actually need the job. Perhaps also a touch better than the average person already working there (if you can get to see them leaving work at some stage).

You may feel a little awkward parading around in a suit, if you don't normally wear one. As you will need to feel comfortable at interview, wear your attire a few times beforehand to get the feel for it and to avoid the need to constantly adjust and fiddle with ties, lapels, buttons, cuffs and the like.

Hair should be neat and under control. Sometimes technical prowess is all-important, such as for computer programmers, scientists and graphic designers, but most of us need to look neat and presentable and show that we respect how other people perceive us. If you want to bunk all that, go and work for yourself. If you want to be inside the system, you have to accept its codes. You can make your statements of individuality once you're on the payroll.

Shoes. Executive type, cleaned and polished. Simple. No dust, scuffs, worn out heels, tatty laces, slip-ons, pub-wear, moccasin-types, sandals and huge heels. You can get away with more trendy types (within reason) probably so long as you're young enough, they look like they cost a bob or two and they go with your suit and general image.

For the ladies, I would suggest business suit. Longer skirts are also fine. As you go above the knee, you may risk setting the wrong tone. To you this may be fine, but you never know the views of the person you are meeting, so err on the conservative side. Once you've got the job, then you can wear your leather mini and see who complains! A similar argument applies to blouses and shirts. Avoid deliberate distraction. You want them to concentrate on nothing more than your professionalism.

Business-like shoes are not a necessity, but avoid high heels – you want to be comfortable after all. Other than that, dress codes for women are far more flexible than they are for men. I would not recommend excessive make up, though. You should be aiming to create the impression that looking professional comes natural to you. You get the idea.

Speech and Voice

Take an objective look at how you talk. Is your voice loud or hushed? Do you force it out from your throat or boom from low down? Are you monotone or are you prone to, as the French say, 'chanter' (to sing)? Do you have a strong accent or do you spout colloquialisms? To see how clear and confident your voice sounds, you can either record yourself, which is a tad false, or keep an eye out during the course of your normal day for your typical manner. Or you could listen to other people. Then consider the following points:

Learn to speak at a steady pace. BBC radio is perfect for following along to, to get a feel for a good pace. If you think shouting at the TV is daft, wait till someone catches you talking to the wireless! Another approach: people often talk with greater clarity on the phone. If this is you, you have a good model for your interview voice.

See if you need to lower your tone a little as well. When you're up-tight, your voice often gets higher, anyway. Conversely, speaking deliberately lower and slower can relax you, as does breathing from lower down in your chest. It also creates more authority in your voice. Even George Bush went to a speech instructor to rid himself of a high pitch. If the most powerful man on earth can benefit from this, I'm sure it'll work for you, too.

Posture

In the more formal atmosphere of the interview room, you are more likely to sit properly anyway. However, note if you have a tendency to fold your arms or wrap your legs around each other two or three times, or have them pointing at ten-to-two (fellahs!). Or if you wring your hands,

99

fidget a lot, play with your hair, rock back and forth like a lonely chimp, or stare at the ceiling or at your feet. These are all signs of nervousness, restlessness or a lack of confidence.

You should sit upright, hands on your lap to start with, legs or feet lightly crossed and maybe slightly leant forward, but not onto the interviewer's desk.

Look them in the eye, but without staring. If you find this difficult, look at the bridge of their nose. This may take a bit of getting used to, so there's another one to practice with.

Avoid overtly flamboyant gestures with the arms and hands. It's natural to use your hands to emphasise your words, but they shouldn't be speaking for you. Some other body language tips are covered next.

Body Language

This can really get quite interesting and you can learn stuff all the time just by watching people and even by watching television, particularly with the sound down. I don't want to get into lots of psycho-babble here, but to point out a few indicators that will help you project the right impression: one of confidence, assertiveness, alertness and keen interest. These are some common body language messages and what they mean:

- By unbuttoning your jacket, you are subtly exhibiting confidence, a relaxed manner and a readiness to talk.
- Legs tightly crossed, arms folded, chin down, means: "You keep away from me", "I don't trust you", or "You're getting nothing out of me!"
- Shifting in your seat, leaning on your hand, scratching your head, putting your fingers to your face and general fidgeting, indicates discomfort.
- Head slightly tilted to one side and/or leaning slightly forward, means: "I'm concentrating on what you're saying."
- Knuckles under the chin: "I'm interested in what you're saying."
- Chin resting in palm: "I'm getting bored."
- Sitting square on to your interviewer can look slightly antagonistic. Turn your chair to a slight angle before sitting down. Gives you more leg room as well.
- Steepled fingers suggests confidence.
- Rubbing the back of the neck indicates disagreement.

- Putting spectacles on the table: "I'm going to tell you something now and you'd better not disagree", or "I've said all I'm going to say" (particularly if they lean back).
- In presentations, it is often better to move your arms from the shoulders, in gesture and expression. Anything else tends to look half-hearted. Sat down, the opposite is true. Generally, move only your hands. Full arm movements are too aggressive close up.
- Mirroring. This is a method for gaining control of the atmosphere without your interviewer ever knowing. Sales people use it a lot to 'bring out' clients. Say, for instance, your interviewer is leaning forward over his file, or is square on with arms folded, looking at you over his glasses. This is a bit intimidating and you don't like it. First of all, fold your arms also. Subconsciously, this is mildly aggressive and your interviewer may immediately relax his posture a little. If not, then a short while later, unfold your arms. A good point to do it is just after they've finished talking. You unfold just before you speak. It looks natural that way. He is likely to mirror your actions. If not, try again. Do the same to get them to sit back in their chair or whatever.

Mirroring is a more advanced technique. You need to be comfortable with your answers, your listening techniques, your general posture and presentation before you start distracting yourself with these matters. Be aware not to do it too much; it might look like your taking the wotsit!

A few additional points:

- Smile now and then by all means, but don't laugh out loud – it really doesn't fit in an interview situation.

- Rather than make a conscious effort to nod in agreement and make the odd affirmative response at the right points, just be aware if you are doing it too often. You may otherwise find yourself thinking about where and how to slot in the next nod or agreement, rather than actually listening to what is being said.

- Be aware of any habits you might have, such as clearing your throat, pursing your lips, tapping your feet or fingers. It may mean nothing, but it looks like nerves to the interviewer and can be most distracting.

Right, that should do it. Don't want you getting paranoid about every little nuance. If you keep your wits about you, you can manipulate the above points to your advantage. For example, if your interviewer gets you with a tough question, your natural response may be to rub your mouth or fold your arms and tap your lips with a forefinger. This indicates straight away that you're struggling. If you, instead, steeple your fingers and nod slowly, it appears you are merely pausing to give due consideration to an interesting question.

Remember one thing: body language is subtle – beware of over-acting. Exaggeration shows insincerity, which translates as distrust.

Listening

Good listeners are rare. Simply concentrating on the words fails most people, never mind picking up on key points, implications and peripheral issues. Good listeners also give off the appropriate body language that says they are interested in the speaker. If you are not sending a "please continue" message, your speaker may well shut off early or ramble too much in an attempt to create some visible feedback that suggests interest.

Next time you're having a coffee break at work, chatting to a friend or, particularly, in the pub (it's easier with a number of people around), take note both of them and yourself to see how good people are as listeners. These are some of the mistakes made when 'listening':

- Too many "Hmm. Yes. OK. Ah, right. Oh, I see. Uh huh." Done too often, the signal is "You're telling me nothing new here", or "Come on, hurry up, I want to say something now."

- Starting to formulate your answers before the person has finished speaking. I think we're all guilty of this one. You miss half of what was said, don't get the full gist and fail to give eye contact. When you start thinking to yourself, your gaze automatically drifts off to the middle distance – a sure sign that you have started to construct your response and are half switched off.

- Interrupting. When someone has actually finished talking, they give signs. These are:
    - Their gaze shifts back to you.
    - Their head may sink slightly or to one side.

- Their voice lowers a little in tone at the end of the final sentence (unless you come from Belfast or are a modern-speaking Aussie).
- Their hands settle back down, sometimes clasped.
- Their arms may fold.

- Not giving eye contact. Gives the speaker the impression, "I'm boring this person / talking irrelevancies / maybe I should shut up." Exaggerations may creep in to regain supposed lost interest. Important points can be neglected, as the speaker now thinks these are boring or irrelevant. Also leads to interruptions, as you miss the signs of a completed speech (above).

- Finishing the speaker's sentences. OK, you're hearing what they say and are paying attention, but if they're not speaking, it's not their words – and you're not listening. It's also really annoying.

- Pick up on points mid-way. This is probably the commonest conversation killer. The track of the exchange can shift completely with one interruption, never to return. What you have now missed you will never know!

- "Me, me, me." Probably the commonest of all and often used in conjunction with the point above. People just love to, or need to, talk about themselves.

As this is so common, a simple example will illustrate the point. Two blokes talking in the pub, the conversation starts:

"Took the missus for a Cantonese the other night. Our anniversary, y'know. Nice place."
"Oh, yuk! I don't like Cantonese. Too bland and sloppy. Give me a curry any day – the type that glow in the dark and have you wondering if you're going to lose a couple of internal organs the next morning. Best one of all is on the High Street. I went last week with the lads from work. After football it was...", blah, blah, blah.

The poor chap. What was he about to say? Reminisce for a while on his 15 years of marriage? Perhaps the night was a disaster and she threw his ring back at him in a temper. Well, our self-indulgent 'listener' will never know, because he was too keen to talk about himself.

A good listener might ask: "Oh, yeah...Where did you go?...What's Cantonese like, anyway?...How many years is it, now?...Did she get all maudlin on you afterwards?...Did she buy you anything?" and so on. Then you will really get to know the other person. Too often, people are excessively keen to spout off about their own stories.

Effective listening is not that easy. You need to mentally highlight the more important points in a fast-moving conversation, to formulate questions without looking away and appearing to have lost interest and then to keep them under wraps until they finish talking, whilst still listening to the rest of the speech.

The 6 words which help the most here are: Who, What, Where, When, Why and How. These are the initiators of 'open' questions that allow you to burrow to the heart of the matter. For the handful of people who don't know what open questions are, these are the ones that require a full answer, rather than a 'Yes', 'No' or 'Maybe'. You can glean all sorts of information from proper listening and judicious questioning. It takes practice, but you can start today. Works great in social situations as well!

Handling Stress

This can be a clincher, but not one you can really look at during the course of your normal day. Not unless you get the chance to volunteer for a presentation or something. It can mean the difference between a sterling, well-controlled performance and... well... not. So getting a feel for how stress affects you and how best you harness it can be crucial.

As soon as you fear the interview, you've lost. Because then you will be concentrating on not fouling up and on the consequences of failure, rather than on your performance and the requirements for success. That old tale still holds true: lay a 2-foot wide plank on the floor and anyone can walk across it. Straddle the same plank between two 40-storey buildings and you know what you can do with your plank! Yet it is still the same plank and the same task. Only this time, the fear of failure overrides the simple task required to succeed.

In keeping with the philosophy of this book, stress should be treated as a positive. For a start, don't call it stress, call it excitement. Then you can see that what you are about to experience is not to be feared. When taking your driving test, for example, were you about to be grilled and have your every movement put under the microscope? Or were you but half an hour from freedom! Before your interview, you are perhaps an hour from a new job, with more pay and better prospects, closer to home and your family, or whatever. It's not a test anymore; it's a chance to better your life – for good. Now that's exciting. The key is to focus on the benefits of success and not the consequences of failure.

Anxiety and excitement really are two sides of the same coin. When we look at examples of interview questions in chapter 10, an optimistic and positive approach is emphasised. The same applies here. You need to count your blessings:

- You have a great-looking CV. They *want* to talk to you and probably hope they can impress you with the job.
- You are thoroughly prepared in your career knowledge, your objectives, your presentation and your answers.
- These two mean you have already beaten the majority of the competition by default.
- If it turns out you're not impressed by them, you will easily get other, better interviews.

After consulting the following chapter, you will also be more familiar with the types of interview and what to expect. With this knowledge, your impending experience will be less of an unknown – that will help quell your anxiety in itself.

9

Interview Types

There is considerable debate about the effectiveness of interviews. Some swear by them and some curse them. And some simply haven't got a clue. Some say it is too costly in staff time and lost work; others that you stand almost as a good a chance of getting the right person as leaning out of your window and yelling at the first passer-by, "Oi! Yeah, you! Wanna job?" Whatever you may think, everybody uses them, so you're going to have to know how to conduct yourself in them.

The first thing to note is that an interview is always a two-way process. Primarily, you *are* out to sell yourself to a new employer. The interviewer, though, also needs to conduct him or herself appropriately to create the right atmosphere so that you are willing and able to divulge important information. If you are confronting your potential new boss, they must also sell themselves to you and create a good image of the company, in case you are invited back or are made an offer. Personally, I have turned down second interviews because the interviewer was (very) badly prepared, not knowledgeable, excessively officious or even patronising.

It's also about compatibility. You both have to be sure that you are right for the job, that you will get on with your boss or your colleagues and that you have the capability/opportunity to advance. So it's not all one way. That said, it is far more one way if you are not currently working: any port in a storm and all that. Make no mistake, though, unless you happen to strike lucky, you're not going to succeed first time out. And it won't necessarily be your fault – for a number of reasons:

- Like a bad date or bungled lines in the most meticulously rehearsed play, interviews can and do go wrong.
- There are bad interviewers just as there are bad interviewees.
- There are many interview types; the correct medium may not have been chosen.

- There may simply be a better, more qualified candidate than you.
- It may be company policy to advertise externally even though there are strong internal candidates.
- Your interviewer may not be very open-minded. He may simply not like the look or sound of you.

If it wasn't hard enough to co-ordinate your own efforts, some parameters such as these will be out of your control. So winning is never guaranteed. However, knowing this helps to keep it in perspective, keeps your morale up, keeps you focused and keeps you fighting.

You can get an idea if you are in for a fair hearing or not by looking out for the following signs of an impending lousy interview. These are if your interviewer:

- Doesn't have all your notes, is disorganised, keeps being interrupted, hasn't read your CV or needs to keep referring to his own notes, job description/profile in order to find the next question. This will result in a hit-and-miss interview, you won't have a fair and equal hearing, important points may be missed, it will be disjointed and you will not be able to create a good, solid argument for yourself.

- Doesn't respond directly to your answers, doesn't pick up on points you make in your answers or misses the point of your own questions. In other words, he's a poor listener.

- Talks too much. All right, you want to know about the job and the firm you'll be working for, but you can ask such questions at the end. And do you really want to know about all the places he's worked in, the old gaffer and his golf handicap? Again, you want to be able to piece together a sound case for yourself and not have ten-minute intervals between answers.

- Doesn't ask open questions. This is just bad interview technique which doesn't allow you to give flowing answers and build a wholesome picture of yourself.

- Doesn't speak clearly or get his point across concisely. He's probably not confident about his interviewing or about the questions themselves and may have not prepared.

Ask yourself, if you behaved like any of those in an interview, would you last? Er...no. So ditch them, too. How are you going to succeed in your career working for people like that? A poor interview stands a better chance of selecting the wrong person. For you, that means you could blunder into the wrong job or a poor organisation. It may seem idiotic not to grab any offer that comes your way, but if you did, would you only end up going through the same process a year later by making a rash decision now?

So what are the hallmarks of a good interview?

- A quiet, neutral venue for a start. Not the guy's office or the boardroom (these are the person's power bases), open plan sales office (too distracting and not private enough) or the pub (yes, it does happen!).
- It is obvious he's read your CV and also knows the details of the position you're applying for. There may be highlighter marks on your CV and additional notes down the side.
- Plenty of open questions (see chapter 10 for some examples of these).
- Establishes a rapport early on.
- Waits until you've finished speaking before giving the next question.
- Listens and responds to things you say, perhaps interjecting now and then, but only for elaboration of a valid point, not to change the conversation.
- Makes notes. There will be a number of applicants to see. The interviewer will not be able to remember everybody and probably should be reporting back to other people.

How *you* should conduct yourself in the interview we'll discuss in chapter 10. First, let's take a brief look at the types of interview, their relative merits and what you can expect.

The One-to-One

More often than not, this will be the type of interview you come across. It can take many forms.

(i) The informal chat (or so it likes to be portrayed). This is supposed to allow you both to get a good idea of each other in your 'natural habitat'. Not a very likely contingency, I'm afraid. This is still business. This is supposed to be the culmination of weeks of hard and dedicated graft for you and a pivotal point in your career. It is no idle whim for the employer, either – they are betting thousands on getting the right person. And you are both still trying to sell yourselves to one another. It can be a rather forced, unreal scenario and even a tad insulting. After all, it's hard work getting this far. Why should all that effort be trivialised?

(ii) The formal interview is a structured session ("I'll tell you about the job and the firm, then we'll go through your CV" kind of style), with pre-planned questions and with your chance to ask questions at the end. This is the most common type.

Sometimes questions are so pre-planned you'll find some of them irrelevant. The idea is to give everyone a fair hearing, which seems logical. However, everybody's background is different and so some questions can not be applied across the board. This is particularly true where a new position is being created and all kinds of candidates apply, or for positions which can benefit from skills transference, again attracting people from different walks.

Still, as an applicant, you feel obliged to answer and so try to conjure up a reply to all of them. Such generalised questions invariably draw generalised answers. Specifics are preferred. Specific questions will be borne out of your CV. The interviewer will look through your responsibilities and achievements and pick out the issues most relevant to the post and other points that pique his interest. If your answers indicate to the interviewer an approved approach to executing these responsibilities, then there will be a direct relation to your compatibility with the new post.

(iii) The middle ground interview (business like, but make-it-up-as-we-go) is thankfully less common. They can vary greatly in length and so don't give everyone an equal hearing. Being conducted to an ad-hoc agenda, they can easily go awry. Strictly speaking, the interviewer should be in control of the interview, but you may find yourself with some freedom to guide the conversation onto your best topics. To the inexperienced, this can be very disconcerting and, at best, such interviews are a very hit-and-miss affair.

Group Interviews

Being out-numbered in the interview room can appear daunting at first, but they do have distinct advantages:

- You get to meet a broader spread of the employer's people.
- You may get to meet future colleagues.
- You can ask a variety of questions and get an answer from the appropriate person.
- One interviewer can ask while another takes notes, which allows a fuller picture to be gained.
- You get to use body language more effectively. With just one interviewer, you either look at them or around the room, which can't really be helped, but can give the wrong impression. Here, you can switch your gaze, addressing each person to avoid staring whilst keeping constant eye contact and giving the distinct impression you're in control. Also, in a way similar to presenters looking for friendly faces in the crowd to latch on to, you can focus more on the panel member whose disposition you prefer. It's a comfort thing.

Group interviews certainly can be more difficult because there is often no let up in the questions, which can switch from one subject to the next and back again, depending on who's asking. This can make it difficult to create a coherent argument and keep your thoughts in order.

Take your time if you find this happening and try not to show your discomfort or irritation. Each interviewer will no doubt want as much out of you as possible. If things seem to be running away from you, this is, ironically, a good time to relax. A good pause and a request to repeat the question gives the hint that things are getting confusing. Don't take it as your fault – the interview should be structured properly.

Simple actions like these can really boost your confidence when things seem to be getting tight. I once watched a trainee engineer weld two plates together after a brief instruction session. As the piece cooled, he picked it up to admire the finished article. The weld immediately gave way and the welded plate clanged back onto the bench. Just as the gathered crowd prepared to pour scorn, he looked the instructor square in the eye and said, "Didn't teach me very well, did you?" A masterly stroke. Instantly averted all blame and pressure. Sure, when it was all over, he went off and assessed his technique, but at the critical moment, when composure was more important, this firmly placed him in the driving seat. This response enabled him to stay in control. The onus switched back to the instructor to address the issue.

Likewise, it is the interviewer's responsibility to make sure it goes well. If you feel the structure of the interview is preventing you from giving your best, it is not your fault. The traditional anxiety-busting anecdote is to imagine the interviewers on the toilet or something. Whatever enables you to maintain your composure, keep it at the back of your mind ready for use.

Consecutive Interviews

Unusual, I have to say. Seen more at assessment days, where half the staff might turn out to watch the circus! You are likely to be rather ambivalent about these. On the one hand, they can be very tiring, hauling yourself from one grilling to the next. On the other, you will be more relaxed after your first one and you also have more than one chance to shine.

Occasionally, such as when whole teams are being recruited through assessment days, the crowd is gradually whittled down as you progress through interviews and exercises. I can tell you, it's not a pleasant experience being rejected half way through. It's like not being picked to be on *anybody's* side to play football. No one shakes your hand and says goodbye – you're just not invited back into the next round. You try to hold your head up and look bold as you slink away, avoiding the gaze of the survivors. You'll probably only do them once!

Assessment Days

Ask yourself one question: do you think people behave the same in front of a camera as they do in their own homes? Of course not. That's why I believe 'real work situation' tests are far from it. When you're under close and constant scrutiny during exercise sessions, you are never going to 'be yourself.'

Then there's the catalogue of numerical, written, verbal, reasoning and other tests 'designed' to assess your competence against the job criteria. Yeah, right! If you practice Mensa or IQ tests and are good at crosswords you'll romp these – you can probably find such test booklets in the library or second-hand bookstores. Otherwise, you'll only do as well as your O-level schooling tells you to do (sorry! showing my age, there!). They are basic intelligence tests, with the flaw that if you practice at them, your score – and therefore, by implication, your intelligence – will also improve. They rarely have any real bearing on your potential for success in the job. Some of the problems can be so obscure, you are given examples to show what patterns to look for, which kind of defeats the object of requiring the savvy to identify the patterns yourself.

Have a careful read of some job adverts in the local paper and decide for yourself how much real business understanding goes into them. Then imagine how well you can be assessed against the criteria drawn from this vague collection of textbook phrases and management buzz-words. However, as I always advocate looking for the positive, here goes.

Firstly, if you're good academically, you can score highly in these tests and compensate for lesser business experience or hiccups at interview. You may also show yourself to be suitable for other positions within the company.

Secondly, the group exercises (the third part of the day) are often supposed to see how good a team player you are. This means that if you behave as they think a team player should behave, you'll do all right. Such as:

- Define the problem first, then define the objective.
- *Suggest* you plan the exercise first before doing anything else.
- *Ask* who wants to be timekeeper, mathematician, chairperson, scribe, etc.
- *Ask* for reasons behind people's suggested approaches.
- *Ask* others to contribute if they seem to be taking a back seat.
- Make sure tasks are adequately portioned out.
- Attempt to reign in particularly aggressive members of your squad by stating you want others to have a chance to speak and test their ideas, or ask what they themselves think of other people's ideas.
- Keep an eye on the clock and the developing chaos before stamping some authority on proceedings, such as, "Come on, folks, time's getting on, let's do what we have / go with (person's) idea."

It's like being in the chimp-house with pseudo-psychologists observing your behaviour and pretending they can objectively and scientifically analyse what they are looking at.

Most of them get it out of books anyway, recite it from the corporate training file or get it from some generic solution provider. This means the same tests do the rounds year after year up and down the country, with different test levels for different entry levels.

What they fail to realise is that this predictability means you can practice this stuff, research it and read about it in books like this. Knowing this blows the whole gaff and boosts your confidence – and that's one of the greatest assets you can take to any interview

So, yes, you're right – it's an act. Besides, who behaves like that when the phone is ringing, the work is piling up and deadlines are pressing? Will your colleagues also have passed these tests and play according to these standards? And who has ever had a boss that tolerates, understands or has time for such mincing about?

More to the point, this kind of approach to team work only usually works in groups of people of equal rank, with equal capabilities and an equal goal, such as shop floor teams and kaisen teams. Often, teams are more "project groups" and consist of a mix of people with particular talents and tasks. Such groups go through various stages of forming, as each member finds a space for their own personality and style in the collective psyche. In other words, *any* approach can be complimentary to the overall team effort. But how many recruitment personnel have studied psychology, team dynamics and personality functions?

Enough, already. In assessment days, more important than getting the tasks completed is that you, personally, are seen to display the correct behaviour. Jump through a few hoops, stuff the square pegs through the square holes and tap the sequence of buttons that gets the reward. If you get all the gold stars and get the job, who cares? It's only for a few hours.

Assessment days do, however, have two redeeming features. They assess how people *might* behave under pressure and certainly how well they can concentrate and for how long. This applies more to the tests than to the exercises, so this quality is not scored equally across the board. The other is that it gives people who are always bad at interviews a chance to get noticed. Nevertheless, interviews *are* crucial. I strongly recommend you practice.

One word of caution. Whatever they may say on the day, you are never immune from scrutiny, even during drink and meal periods. No alcohol or bad manners, please, and try to avoid stuffing yourself – you'll be nodding off afterwards. People are always too polite to polish everything off, so you will no doubt get the chance for seconds later. Time it right and you can get to exchange a few words with one of the interviewers or assessors, get friendly and perhaps raise the odd question concerning the company or the job. Be sensible in your comments, be professional, play the game and enjoy the day.

Agency Interviews

Dealing with agencies was covered in chapter 7. Your CV preparation will usually be adequate here, as these interviews are far more about matching your qualifications and experience to the post than the softer elements, assessment of such will be the duty of the organisation themselves.

It is the agent's job to filter all the applicants and send in only those with a good chance of getting the job. This can be viewed in two ways: people who are eminently qualified and people who are maybe not so academically endowed but who are good at selling themselves. It can take a while for inabilities or incompatibilities to show through, but as long as the vacancy stays filled for a few months, the agent gets paid in full. This may be another reason why you do not land a job to which you thought you were more than suited. The only people that can really know this are the recruiters themselves – assuming, that is, that they are aware of precisely what is influencing their decisions!

10

Clinching The Deal

The whole job search program is a selling process. It's a job *market*. You identify prospective clients (employers), you determine that your product (you) fits their needs (job profile, nature of business), you make your pitch (you outline 'what's in it for them' through your CV and approach letters), they buy into it and then make you an appointment to visit (the interview). This is where we stand now. This is where you clinch the deal.

Be aware that good preparation will put you ahead of most candidates before you even turn up. Your CV has organised relevant thoughts concerning your career and your preparation from previous chapters will have you projecting yourself in a controlled, assertive and professional manner. This will all make life in the interview room so much easier, not least because you know you've covered all the angles. It will boost your confidence and that is a big plus in any interviewer's note book. All you need to do now is stay focused for the task in hand. So let's look at how you sell yourself face-to-face to achieve this.

The Preparation

How you now prepare in the time leading up to the interview depends upon what suits you best. Sometimes you will be given a choice of times or dates to attend. Pick the one you prefer. If you're a morning person, get an early appointment, but do try to avoid city rush hours. It can make your arrival time a bit of a lottery and not have you in the best mood for the task in hand. If you don't come round till midday and need half a gallon of caffeine to kick start the old grey matter, then get an afternoon appointment.

Some things you ought to do in the days leading up are:

1. Get the names and titles of the people who will be interviewing you. You don't want to be trying to pick them up on the day. Incidentally, don't be put off by titles. It is a form of power, but once you recognise that, it loses impact. A one-man band can call himself a director. It doesn't mean anything.

2. Confirm the time, date and location (like any other meeting). Ask for a map of how to get there and check it in your road atlas. If it's not clear, call them back to confirm. You don't want to be fighting a one-way system ten minutes before you're due in. It's a great feeling to get there first time, no hassle, in plenty of time, park up, stroll up and sign in. It allows you to adapt to your new environment, get used to the surroundings and allow any stresses of driving to subside.

3. If you are late, do your best to telephone them with an ETA. With the best intentions, I've been scuppered by one-way systems, road-works, traffic jams, tube strikes, no-one at the public information desk, mis-reading the address, car faults, the works. Everyone knows travel these days is a nightmare, so they should be sympathetic. Look on the bright side – you'll have something to talk about when you arrive.

4. Don't drink beer the night before. It's amazing how long it can linger and you want to be as clear as a Tibetan monk's conscience for the morning.

5. Always carry mints or a mouth freshener spray. I recommend this to anyone in business. There's no shame in it, but there is if you're breathing coffee, greasy breakfast fumes or cheese and onion sandwich all over your host! They're unlikely to say: "Would you like a mint imperial? Are you quite sure?", but it will certainly distract their attention and probably create a bad sub-conscious image of you.

6. From the above list, make your own list of things to take. Include an extra copy of your CV and any company literature you have. Don't take your interview preparation notes or practice questions. If they're not internalised by the time you set off, an extra few minutes isn't going to help and you will only end up confusing yourself. You should, however, be able to rehearse them to yourself as you drive or travel.

A good night's sleep is also essential. So try to get up rather earlier than normal the day *before* the interview. That way, you can be confident of being tired enough to overcome the adrenaline and a racing mind to sleep well that night and emerge alert on the interview day. I would avoid eating too much before setting off, but take a snack or some confectionery for the journey. A half-hour walk before leaving may help to clear your head and gather your thoughts. Take some water and some mints or a breath-freshener spray.

Once you arrive, you need to focus. Everyone now seems to advocate relaxation before the interview, to take deep breaths, close your eyes for while. If that's your medicine, take it by all means. Personally, I don't go for that. I believe it's OK to be nervous. You should be. When we talked about handling stress before, I mentioned that it should be viewed positively, that you should start by calling it 'excitement'. The key is to channel your excitement and make it work for you. Look at it this way: by focusing on how nervous you're trying *not* to be, you automatically make it worse. Saying to yourself "don't be nervous, don't be nervous" precisely focuses on what? ...being nervous. A quick test: right now, I want you <u>not</u> to think of your left foot!

What did you think of? Your left foot? Likewise, what happens if someone says, "Don't drop it!"? You get all uptight about dropping the thing. All you can think about is the dire consequences of failing.

Fact is, there's nothing wrong with being nervous. A gibbering wreck, maybe. But if your mind isn't racing and your palms aren't sweaty, you've done something wrong: you don't care about what you're doing, you're not too bothered about the job and you're not challenging yourself. This is your examination. This is what you have revised over and over for. But having done all that revision, you just *know* you are going to pass. It's the wait that's the most anxious moment, not the exam itself.

As you wait for interview, you should be gearing yourself up, like an athlete waiting for the gun, thinking about their technique, their aim time and the finish line. Look for things to tie yourself in with your surroundings, for clues as to the organisation you are visiting: the class of car in the car park, the nature of the reception area – is it too formal, too extravagant, is this *is* where your bonuses will be going?! It's tempting to quiz the receptionists, but they are rightly very evasive on any company matter and they are usually busy. Glance through the company literature and try to leave time to rehearse some key answers, remind yourself of names, how you should present yourself, sit and speak, your "front talk" (see later) and so on. All this time, you are limbering up, keeping your mind alert. You can relax all you like when it's over.

Done in a controlled manner, rather than allowing your emotions to run amok and getting all giddy, you may well find that the actual interview situation is easier than you thought. With all your preparation, you'll easily break the ice, go through your introduction routine and settle into the role. Then you will relax – naturally and not forcedly or feel under duress to do so.

The Greeting

If you've prepared correctly, you'll remember the names of the people you're meeting. As you're introduced, look them in the eye and repeat their names back to them with a firm shake of the hand. Job's a good 'un. Already, you're attentive, polite and professional.

As you enter the room, wait to be told where to sit. The interviewer may want you in a particular place for his own comfort or so all present can see and talk to you properly. Apart from that, it's polite. Don't be afraid to move the chair a little. Pull it back from the desk to give yourself a bit of room, turn it slightly to avoid a direct, square on, confrontational position. Too often I have plonked myself precisely where the chair was, whacked my shin against a cross beam underneath, found myself resting my arms on *his* desk and had to move back half way through anyway, just to cross my legs. Make yourself comfortable and give yourself your own space. You need to be at your best.

You can't expect the interviewer to remember everything. So feel free to take your coat off, ask for a blind to be pulled if the sun is in your eyes or for some water if it is in the room and so on.

Also, place any handbags or cases by your side at your feet and not on the interviewer's desk. If someone offers you a drink, take it. Water is best – you don't want coffee-breath – and it'll give you something to handle for comfort, to soften a dry mouth and to fill in a pause while you think.

The Introduction

Ideally, your interviewer should have collected you first. If they are relaxed and confident, they will engage you in a little "front talk" as you enter the room and take your seat. If they're a little quiet, chances are they're nervous, so you can now take some of the initiative to build your confidence by opening the front talk yourself.

Front talk is ice-breaking chit-chat. But with a purpose. It helps to establish a rapport between strangers and, hopefully, establish some common ground. Again, salesmen do it all the time. If you ever invite one round to your house, they will instantly look around the room for photographs, pictures, signs of pets or small children, anything to strike up a pre-business conversation that has direct interest to the client and makes the visitor appear friendly.

I have a photograph above the fireplace, which I took, of mist rising out of the South Pennine valleys. It immediately catches their attention. I tell them it's Borneo or somewhere and listen to the garbage they come out with as they try to make up a conversation about a place they've never even seen on a map.

There are some subjects to avoid, though. Avoid comments about family or spouses – you're treading on personal and potentially dodgy ground there. Mementos are good, souvenirs, trophies, charity certificates and the like; so is the view from the window (without getting flippant). However, always ask a simple question first, to test the water before diving in. On one occasion, as a consultant, my colleague noticed a picture of a Spitfire on the office wall and immediately started banging on about how great they were and had he been to the war museum in Leeds and such like. Then the guy kindly informed him that all that stuff bored the crap out of him and the picture actually belonged to someone he shared the office with. Boops! Get out of that one, Rommell!

With the pleasantries now over, it is, unfortunately, time to get down to business. To give you a head start in what follows, let's take a look at some typical interview questions. I strongly recommend you look at this next section thoroughly and practice your own answers over and over in your head. If I could insist, I would! Then have a go at devising your own questions, based upon your particular history. Even if you think you are a natural at this, you want to work on being concise and to the point and not risk fumbling about for good examples or the best way of explaining yourself when you're on the spot.

Great Answers to the Hardest Interview Questions

Listed below are some highly likely candidates for interview questions. Some of these can be real toughies – if, that is, you're not prepared. You'll notice that they are fairly general in nature. General questions are often the hardest to answer, since you have to think creatively on the spot to come up with a relevant answer. For example, if I asked you "What did you do last year?", would you immediately know where to start? Bit tricky. Compare that with the question, "Tell me about your holidays" and you see the difference. The area of reference is narrower; your thoughts are immediately channelled. Your preparation comes in very useful for such questions, as we shall see. Read through these questions carefully and you'll get a better feel for it. As always, be positive.

Q *Tell me about your current job.*
A Your CV will already have good examples of what you did – and did well. Start by stating your chief responsibilities. This will help categorise your thoughts and give you a short mental list to work through. Add what you liked about each, how you made progression in each of them or how you improved the lot of the company. Don't harp on about the bits you disliked or the people you wanted to punch, however tempting it is.

It's OK to be critical as long as it's constructive criticism. For example, "I thought that project was badly planned. Then again, it was the project manager's first and she wasn't afraid to ask for support. And we know where we went wrong."

An answer like this can leave you open to more questioning, such as, "Where did you go wrong, then, and what did you do to prevent those mistakes in future?" Now, if you're good, selecting for yourself answers like the one above can lead into areas where you can shine. If you made a real contribution to supporting the project manager, you are now leading the interviewer (unbeknown to him) onto your home ground, where you can bring to light all your initiatives in the project and how they helped matters.

Q *What motivates you?*
A Unless you're going to be a stockbroker, IFA or consultant, avoid saying "money", even though it's true! It's not usually politically astute to be so blunt about this kind of thing. Instead, you might

mention things like seeing the production figures rising, or knowing that you've made a positive difference to someone's life through your counselling skills, advice or training. You will probably find useful ideas in your 'key accomplishments list'.

Take ProFile's CV service, for instance. Why not? Although making big bucks is the name of the game (if only!), we only make money if our clients achieve success out of us. Then we get referred or recommended and the business grows. To get a referral or a letter back from a satisfied client is a real buzz. It means we've hit a winning formula. So, although business growth is the key issue, it only derives from customer success, so that is the issue to quote.

Q *What contributions do you think you could make to this position?*
A Refer back to your CV, pick out your successes and key responsibilities and apply them to the new job description. Obviously, there should be directly compatible skills, otherwise you wouldn't be there. This will give you loads to talk about. Refer back to the section on skills transference to see what else you can come up with.

There may be others, too, not directly implied in the job description. For example, you realise that the employer has reduced its workforce recently. This may mean motivation has dropped and team working is required. Your people-management skills and team-building experience could be useful here. Perhaps there are new people on board, in which case your training and coaching experience would be useful.

Q *Why are you leaving your current job?*
A There could be loads of reasons, but pick the least controversial one. Is it a lack of opportunity? Is the business going downhill (as long as it's not your fault!)? Is it unchallenging and in what way? Are you consciously changing career and why? Do you want promotion or more responsibility? If asked, compare the two roles. Show you have assessed your current situation and have an eye to the future, you have ambition and you are willing to break out and fulfil it. Do give the impression, though, that you're not about to move on again in a hurry and that you intend to be around for a good time yet, regardless of whether you actually will be or not.

Q *Why were you out of work for so long?*

A An unimportant question at the end of the day. People who are returning to work have a ready answer here. Otherwise it's a good chance to admit you're not perfect and get it out of the way. Perhaps you were in a lousy relationship and had to first get out to find the freedom to get back to work. You could say your job-hunting technique was poor, you recognised you needed assistance and you weren't afraid to ask for some, so you made a modest investment in this book and hey-presto!

Q *Your a _(role)_ already. Do you think you should be looking for a higher position now?*

A Maybe you are, maybe you're not. If you're not, say why. Perhaps you have too many home responsibilities or you prefer to use your wealth of experience to coach others. Or explain how the job has changed in recent years and still keeps you interested. In either case, show that there are things you are still learning or are keen to learn.

You could also compare the new job description to your old one and highlight added responsibilities or challenges. For example, in the time that I was a shift manager, the role changed out of all recognition. Instead of being a fire-fighter, supervisor and general dogsbody, later roles focused on health and safety, quality, inter-departmental projects, training, coaching and building self-managed teams. It was the same title, but the responsibilities had shifted up a few notches.

Alternatively, you could admit that you're still honing your skills in your current position, ready for a move up. At the moment, you want to broaden your experience and the chance to be in an expanding company, where you will have a better opportunity to apply yourself. This shows a keen interest to progress and advertises that you intend to stick around for a good while.

Q *What did you like about your last job?*

A Similar to the "what motivates you" question. If you can come up with stuff that is also part of the new job objective and the job requirements, then it is plain you will also like your new job. Only refer to actual work examples, to back up your reasons, if you are pressed further. The more you say, the more you may be pressed and the more justification you will have to come up with.

Q *What did you dislike about your last job?*

A Being positive here might seem like total contradiction, but it can be done. Don't say you hated your boss, say there was a difference in style. You prefer the face-to-face approach of marketing development, spending time with customers, talking to sales, etc; your boss preferred the structured, research-based, paperwork approach with formal presentations. At least then, you had two approaches to the same issues and so a more comprehensive picture.

The point about finding issues relevant to the new job applies here, too. IT, for example, is often a key development issue. If you were a little frustrated by your old employer's lack of verve in IT matters, you could express your interest in using office software to facilitate daily operations. If you felt you lacked management support in your previous role, express this as a keen interest in training and development. If you hated all the paperwork, say that this could have been done by someone at a lower grade, freeing you to take on more challenging duties. Perhaps you believe in the power of teamwork. Your current place doesn't even have daily meetings, so they're missing out on experience, information, problem identification and opportunities for continuous improvement. This allows you to get back to positives again, such as the training you have in mind, the prospects at the new employer and so on.

Q *How do you get on with your boss?*

A "She's clever. I've learnt a lot. Perhaps gets into a flap too often. Then again, she has more responsibility than me." Answers like these show a positive, objective attitude as well as empathy and understanding.

If you didn't get on too well or if your boss was elusive or conspicuous by their absence, you could explain how you believe that your seniors should be there to provide support and guidance, as you do for those whom you supervise or work with.

There is nothing wrong with this answer as it stands, as it shows your team spirit, but it does contain a sense of criticism, which will be probed further. In which case, avoid giving examples of your criticism; this will only provoke antagonism. Instead, explain your belief in team-work, a supportive environment and how you believe you should be able to approach your seniors to learn as much and as quickly as possible. This is far more positive and displays a progressive energy. Try to do it as concisely as possible; getting into discussions about other people can be rather dodgy ground.

123

Q *How do you get on with those around you?*
A This is actually an easy one. Refer back to some figures and accomplishments on your CV. As a manger, these will speak for themselves. If you worked in a team, it is unlikely you could cite such successes if you hadn't gelled. Talk about the positive meetings you have each day, perhaps how you socialise or if you have a special understanding and working relationship with someone.

Q *Where do you see yourself in five year's time?*
A Do I look like Russell Grant? Seriously, this *is* a serious question. They want to know if you have a personal battle plan. Typically, clear visions of the future are the domain of the wealthy and successful. But that's another story. For most of us, it's hazy or vague at best. "I want to be a director", "I want to be two places higher" or "I want to be in charge of my own department" doesn't cut it.

To make it easier and to avoid them asking really awkward questions about something you're probably speculating on, I would avoid real specifics here. But you should be able to spell out your immediate plans. Something like, "Well, it'll take a good year or so to get a grasp of my new role. After that, I would like to be looking to expand into such-an-area or train in whatever. After that, I'll have to see how I perform in a more senior role, but I'd certainly like to move into IT or European marketing or whatever."

In reality, no one is going to make you sign a declaration of intent based on what you say, so you can afford to be a little "adventurous" in your ideas. In five years' time, who's going to remember? Who's going to hold you to it? Who will still be around? Will you? Will the business be the same? Hardly. Times will have changed and so will have your plans. All you need to do is to come up with some sort of action plan that, based on you, the new firm and the new job, fits in with the general scheme of things.

Q *What are your weaknesses?*
A Here's a noose, put your head in it! Actually, there a loads of ways you can get out of this one. Just don't go for the clichéd "I'm a perfectionist" crap. Come up with something that isn't going to make them wince and which can also be taken positively. Impatience, for example – "I like to see results, it keeps me motivated". This wouldn't work for a counsellor or a teacher, of course, you'd have to come up with your own. Or maybe, "I prefer to plan things through; most

people tend to jump in with a "we'll cross that bridge later" attitude. Creates problems, I think."

Whatever you say, you can be sure the interviewer will try to look at it negatively and see how you get round that one. If you said "impatience", he may reply, "Wouldn't that just annoy people? Do you have a problem with people who are not quite as bright as you? Don't you believe you should plan things through properly?" "Au contraire," you say. "You need a spread of people to make an effective team." And then you say how your style complimented the overall team spirit and how the team results speak for themselves.

Conversely, if you mentioned meticulous planning, you may be accused of holding people back. You can respond as above and maybe add how you prevented mistakes that would have taken much longer to rectify than through effective pre-planning.

Neither of these examples is disastrous and both can be construed in a positive sense by the interviewer. All they are looking for is some rational thought, not scientific, irrefutable fact.

If you prefer, you can be more blunt about it. Anything you own up to in response to this question will not be in your favour. That doesn't make any sense, so decline. Besides, you don't dwell on your weaknesses, anyway.

You may still be pressed for an answer, in which case you can revert to one of the above answers or get a little more intellectual and philosophical, viz. Strengths and weaknesses are relative. What works in one situation may not work in another; what was once a good approach may soon no longer work. On top of that, you will not be working alone. No-one can do everything, but as a group or a team you should be able to work together to capitalise on individual strengths and to compensate for and overcome whatever weaknesses you each may have.

If that's a little verbose for you, there is a quicker way out. If you're currently learning something new, you can profess to being less than satisfactory in this matter, which is why you took the initiative to improve. Here's a good one: I once worked with a German woman who said she didn't think her English was up to scratch. What else could the interviewer say except, "It seems alright to me."?

Q *What are your strengths?*
A Here's a pedestal, a megaphone and a harlequin jacket covered in flashing lights. Go for it. Trouble is, most of us get shy when given this sort of opportunity. We're not used to boasting about ourselves. To make it easier, pick out your core competencies. These are often the '-ing' words we talked about in chapter 6: team-building, computing, programming, counselling, listening, analysing, etc.

If you prefer a more subtle approach, you can suggest it is difficult to be subjectively critical or that blatantly praising yourself leads to complacency. In other words, you prefer to stay objective and keep learning. However, you are, in fact, the best in your department at whatever or have been doing such-and-such for x-number of years and have been promoted on merit to this level. Perhaps people come to you for advice on this, that and the other, so these must be recognised strengths of yours. Now, instead, you are being objective about your achievements, rather than simply blowing your own trumpet and are reflecting on other people's *recognition* of your strengths, rather than your own opinion.

Q *What has been your biggest mistake?*
A You can pick anything here – except for getting married, getting arrested and dropping your trousers at the last office party. Whatever you come up with, you <u>must</u> have an explanation ready of how you made sure you never made that goof again.

Those are the tougher, general questions you are likely to encounter. Anything else will be CV-related and therefore a doddle to handle. Some important points to remember about answering questions are:

1. Face-to-face, enthusiasm is probably the one thing that all interviewers look for. As is a positive attitude, which is why it has featured so prominently throughout this book. You don't have to be a David Bellamy or a Magnus Pike – it's a good idea to keep your gestures under control, anyway – but keen interest and optimism, as the above examples exhibit, can add an extra spark to all your answers.

2. You'll notice that some of the above responses are quite short. You don't need to give long explanations to every question, particularly the ones where you are being asked about your opinion of other

people – this can be a real quagmire. The more you say, the more there is to pick up on and the more likely you are to trip yourself up.

3. If you get a question you have no answer to, admit it has never been in your job to date. Ideally have a relevant side issue or be able to show an interest in it. For example, I can't speak a second language, but I did once go to the work's evening classes. It was difficult being on shifts, so I bought a book and dictionary instead. I never used them, but they don't know that. If you do get one you can't answer, say so. You'll look dafter if you start making stuff up and talking cobblers. A good tactic is to ask the interviewer to rephrase the question, or say you're not quite clear what is meant. It gives you time to think and maybe a re-wording will trigger some sort of answer.

   In any case, an interviewer will not dwell on an issue if you are clearly struggling. They know as well as anyone that interviews are stressful and time is short. They, too, want you at your best to encourage you to keep talking. They don't want you shrivelling up. So be assured, any difficult bits will soon pass.

4. Wherever possible, keep you answers relevant to the job you seek, rather than giving long history lessons and personal stories. Your résumé has been created in this manner. It says to prospective employers that, based on your stated job objective, this is what you can do to prove you're up to the job. The same goes for your interview answers.

5. Remember, as a self-managed employee, you take full responsibility for your own career. Blaming it on others is not in your repertoire and it turns interviewers off, so keep such comments strictly out.

6. Look at your résumé or the examples given in chapter 3 and see how specific they are. Similarly, in your interview, avoid generalistic phrases like "I'm good with people", "I'm experienced in..." or "I've always fancied doing...". Be specific: give reasons, examples, numbers. Then they get a good picture of your capabilities and a firm grasp of what you're about and where you are going.

7. You may not have great answers to every question, but any reasonable answer is better than shrugging your shoulders. Half the

battle is showing that you are confident, coherent and able to think. Really, you're just very well prepared.

8. Most importantly, don't waffle. Be concise. Stick to the point of the question. If you find yourself digressing into long examples, you're starting to get off track and may be about to put your foot in it. You risk turning it into your own therapy session and rambling on without really thinking.

9. Another common mistake relates to confirmation. You see this often in presentations and meetings. Someone makes a point, then looks around at a collection of apparently blank faces. So they repeat what they've just said from another angle or with more examples or embellishments. In reality, it's not that the audience doesn't understand, it's just they're digesting what has been said, are considering a reply or agree entirely with the comments made. When you've given your answer, don't expect the interviewer to respond immediately. Don't think you have to fill any 'awkward' silences. If you do feel the urge, ask if you're making sense. If the interviewer is not sure, they will say so or pick up on something you said.

That's quite a lot to take in, but at last the deal is nearly struck. You now need to gather your wits and recall some of your questions for the interviewer. Bear in mind that by now, their minds are more than likely made up. In fact the first few minutes would have been critical. That is why so much of this book is dedicated to preparation and to the pre-interview build up. So what follows is of secondary importance, but necessary nonetheless and allows you to better determine your own opinion of your prospective employer.

Your Questions For Interviewers

At the end of the 'interrogation', you will get the chance to turn the tables and see what the interviewers have got to say for themselves. You must have at least some, but not reams of questions. Stick to a few central issues for your first interview. Detailed stuff can wait for when you are called back.

The best questions you can ask will be based upon things you've picked up during the interview. But this takes a certain skill and composure. It's easier to take a few in with you. A simple and effective method is to memorise one key word from each question you have. Say, for example, you have identified from the career potential that you will eventually want to develop some new competencies (training), that you know the company has been restructured (company direction) and that you know structured internal communications are paramount to effective management. So you ask about Communications, Training and Strategy - CaTS for short. Even easier to remember.

There are plenty of fillers to use as well, to give you a more rounded impression of the organisation.

- *Why did the last person leave? How long were they in the job?*
  Empty answers like "He just upped sticks and left" are suspicious. No one leaves perfectly good employ without a damn good reason. If they got promoted, you could be on to a winner. Ask what he or she does now, then find them and talk to them. They could be your best and probably only reference.

- *The people I will be working with, do they have similar backgrounds to me?*
  If you're way more qualified than the others are, you could be in for a frustrating time and you may be below your station. Perhaps you'd be better off with people on your own level, with whom you can work quickly and share experiences, or perhaps people from whom you can learn.

- *Do you have ideas of how the position will develop and what may be expected of me in years to come?*
  They ask you for your five-year plan; ask them for theirs. Many firms boast that they recruit for two positions higher, but few can say what those two positions will be or why such opportunities will occur (impending retirement, expansion plans, etc.). They just have a vague notion that they want a highly competent person for an average job. A clued-up firm will know that, with some extra training to build on your current abilities, you could be up for promotion in a specified field, though not necessarily a particular post, and will be able to explain this.

- *Do you have any reservations about anything we have discussed so far?*

129

This can be a wonderful closing question. It can also be a bit of a waste of time and leave you feeling like you've pushed it a bit too far. They may look unsettled and say 'No'. It could mean they haven't yet summarised your qualities. It could also be an evasive answer. It could mean they don't want to say "you've got no chance, mate" to your face and now you've really put them on the spot. Good interviewers will point out a few things that have occurred to them. This gives you a final chance to plug any gaps, by repeating some points or including a few extras you'd omitted before.

You will need to prepare this last response carefully. Avoid simply repeating yourself over again, for they will be thinking, "Yes, I know, you've told me once!" If you have a few extra examples of the key issues in reserve, now is the time to bring them out. But don't make your response too long, though. As far as the interviewer is concerned, the interview is over. If, however, the interviewer starts up again, you have hit a good point. Adopting a more conversational tone in this final part will help. Sit back in your chair and 'open up'. You want to project a message along the lines of, "I agree with you. But let's be honest for a minute here... I do have a greater understanding and experience of this matter than has been covered in this limited time. And I can quote an example or two and explain how it ties in with my other abilities."

It is important not to disagree with the interviewer here. You must first agree and then turn him around. This is another negotiating and sales tactic designed to overcome resistance. Say, for example, your interviewer is expressing disinterest in daily meetings for teams (takes too much time, lost production, etc). You first of all agree that, improperly chaired, they can degenerate into little more than extended coffee breaks. But with good management support, they can be a valuable investment of time and be a useful vehicle for continuous improvement, actually improve productivity and free up management time. By simply starting with an "Oh, absolutely, I agree..." response, you are not being directly antagonistic and so avoid turning the other person off.

It is sometimes suggested that you can ask if you are going to be recommended for a second interview. This depends on the position. It may be a good question for a sales job, because you're expected to go for leads, recommendations and seek closure. Most times you'll get the answer, "Well, I can't say for sure, yet, because I haven't seen everybody.

But we've had a good discussion here, I think it's gone well. I'll be in touch." So you're none the wiser. On the whole, I'd leave it out.

A couple of final points. Avoid questions to do with hours of work, salary, bonuses, cars and such like. All this will be on the contract sent with the job offer. If you don't like them, you are under no obligation to sign. Such matters are covered in more detail in the next chapter.

And finally, if you get the opportunity for a site tour, try to avoid it. If your guide is a peer or an independent, rather than your boss, volunteer for a cup of tea and a chat instead. Then grill them about life there. There are many poor organisations out there and you should do your best to avoid them. Getting into the wrong one can be costly in terms of motivation, finances, lost career time and the state of your CV. When your time is nearly up, ask your guide for a quick tour through the site and to point out just a few important areas. Then you can at least pass a few comments on the place and perhaps ask a couple of well-placed questions when you return.

11

After The Event

At last you can breathe out, but it's not quite over yet. While it is all still fresh, you need to critique your performance. Sometimes it is very hard to remember much about an interview. But if you can, it's a good idea to jot down a few notes immediately afterwards about questions you couldn't answer, things they said and issues that were covered with particular interest. These will come in handy if you're invited back a second time, as you can prepare for likely areas of interest.

If it turns out you were not successful, feel free to ask why. This is a good way to fine tune your skills, improve your answers, or pick better job ads if there clearly wasn't a suitable match this time. It's better to give your interviewer some advanced warning of this, so that they can be prepared. Either ask their secretary to pass a message on that you will call at a later and convenient date, or write a letter. Friendly, chatty tones are OK for these. Say that you understand their decision and that you are simply looking to improve for next time. You may disagree with some of the things you hear (but not to them, though!), which is OK. Misunderstandings do occur and you are also assuming that the interviewer had a complete and logical understanding of what makes the ideal candidate and that the interview was comprehensive. Not always the case.

Whatever happens, you mustn't dwell on it. Remember: "High commitment; Low attachment." You have others to attend to now. Trait 3 in chapter 5 says learn from your mistakes. A positive critique of your interview is the way forward. Stay optimistic. Eventually, you *will* crack it.

Break Out The Cream Cakes!

You've got the offer! ...pending medical report and references, naturally. References are a ubiquitous requirement, but of distinctly dubious value. There are serious flaws in the logic of obtaining references. Before you research your history, you should research your historian. Yet employers seek the opinion of people they have never met, know nothing about and have no idea as to their qualities or competencies.

Very few people get fired for incompetence. Mostly it's redundancy, which is largely the fault of the very people they are asking. And yet they still ask these senior people for their opinion. What is the point of asking business-related questions to someone who is running a failing business? If they are poor business people themselves, how can they possible judge others? And what right do they have? Bizarre.

There's not a lot you can do about this, mind, except to point out this logic if you feel the need – with a little more diplomacy, of course. If they do give you a bad reference, it's likely to be taken as gospel. If you give your old employer a bad write up, you'll be frowned upon. And what if you're leaving for a better post and they don't want to lose you? Will you get a glowing reference or will they try to scupper your chances? Politics, eh? Who knows? Ever wondered how the worst of the bunch gets promoted to another department while the best stay put? Well, would you want to keep a duffer in your team and let the good ones go?

Whatever. Don't quit your old job until your new one is in the bag, signed and sealed. And don't just sign any old contract, either. You are perfectly free to change any condition you don't like. If you want 25k and not 22k, relocation expenses and one month's notice instead of three, say so. Write a covering letter specifying your changes and send back the contract. They may then say the terms are standard company policy. Either rubbish, laziness or they're just trying it on. Mind you, not everything is negotiable. Things like medical cover and pension contributions really will be company-wide issues. If you do want some details changing, you may find yourself in negotiations. This is an extensive subject I can't really do full justice to in this book, but I will certainly give you a few pointers.

Some Negotiating Tips

Negotiations are not about right and wrong, they are about strength of position. You should already have ideas about the prestige of the position, the responsibility involved, the likely hours and the potential they see in you. Comparing this to your last post and other similar positions you have seen in the course of your job hunt will help you gauge your case. Generally, you have greater bargaining power:

* The higher up the organisation you are.
* You have more than one potential offer.
* You are already working.
* Time is on your side (the employer needs you quick).
* The job is new or rather unique (there are no directly comparable terms).
* You know what the going market rate is for the job.
* You know what other people in the organisation are on.
* You are sure you are being recruited for higher things.
* You have identified several issues, other than salary, which you can barter about (more on this below).
* You have particular expertise they want.

So how do you capitalise on such points of leverage? Here are a few techniques.

The Trade Off
This is rule Numero Uno. Whenever you agree to something, ask for something else in return:
  "I'm used to having a company car. Without one, I'll need an extra 10% to cover the travelling."

Pah!
Always balk at the first offer. A simple turn or lowering of the head, a frown, a sigh or a look of disdain will do it. Then you need to return by stating your expectations. On the subject of which...

Fortune Favours The Brave
Always ask for more than you want, as you will always be bartered back. Have a range in mind, ask for your top figure, settle for somewhere in the middle, but never go below your bottom figure. You would be better off

walking away than seeming to cave in to a ridiculous offer. That just sets a precedent for your future pay rises and any future jobs you go for.

The Red Herring

There is usually more to it than salary: relocation costs, car, bonuses, medical cover, pension contribution levels, etc. Decide which of these are important to you and which aren't. Then you make out the opposite. Say they refuse to give you a car, which you're not really bothered about anyway. You then make a real issue of it. You bemoan the initial outlay of getting your own, the MOT, insurance and repair worries and maybe the lost prestige and so on. A company car has real value to you. "But," you say, "if I can't have one, I suppose I could settle for a three thousand extra a year. It's not the same, but still." So you get maybe two thousand, which was your aim all along.

You're not lying about anything here, just doing business (My Co. is looking to increase its profits) and this is standard business practice. You are preying on your opponent's lack of information. And information is power. Business *is* a battle. And as the Ancient Chinese military strategist, Sun Tzu explains, "War is the art of deception."

Plead Ignorance

If they are pushing a point you don't like, or if you are trying to press one home yourself, it's not always necessary to keep up the arguments. Pleading ignorance as to their objections can sometimes lead to it being dropped or traded.

"I simply can't understand what your objection is."

"I hear what you're saying, but I just don't see your problem."

Walk Away

This is a real toughie! To do this, you either have to have other options open to you, be somewhat experienced (you have to know when the time is right to call this one) or you need brass balls like church bells. This is probably the most powerful technique of all. If you show you are prepared to walk away from the deal, after you have both put so much time and effort in to it so far, then your power base will raise several floors at once.

In the reading list, you will find my preferred reference on negotiating. Consult such a reference and you'll understand these points more.

The problem many people face is believing they are in a weak negotiating position: you are trying to convince them to give you a job and you think the best way to clinch the deal is to cut your price. There are a number of conflicting considerations here:

1. There is always someone else waiting in the wings ready to take your place at a lower price, but are they as good as you?
2. Do you want to jeopardise your chances now, having come this far?
3. Do you want to compromise the integrity of your product – you – by settling for a lower amount?
4. Could you do better elsewhere, or do you take it and be grateful?

Looking at it objectively, you have a great CV, they have been keen to get you in, your CV preparation has prepared you for interview and you have performed well this far. They see your qualities and they're thinking, "This one feels right, I hope he/she accepts." That evens it out somewhat, doesn't it?

If you've been through this material carefully, you will see how strong your position can be when it comes to the crunch. There's no harm in testing the water (Trait 2 – take risks). However, I strongly recommend you do some negotiating study before trying this stuff on. You don't want to risk losing everything for the sake of a few quid if this is the job you really want.

Tips Concerning Salaries

Let's put the above tips to some use and see how you might apply them to getting a decent salary. You'll notice that your résumé doesn't give a salary. This is sometimes used as a way of excluding certain candidates. Opinion is divided on the matter. Some say state it, some say give a range. I would suggest avoiding it altogether until you are offered the post. You will be asked about it then.

Assuming you have assessed the responsibilities within your target job, compared to your current one, you could say something like: "Naturally, I'm looking for career progression over my last/current post. This one has more responsibility and a wider remit, so it should naturally carry a higher salary than I'm currently getting*[(p.137)]. However, career progression is a key issue. I believe I can really develop the role here and there is potential in your organisation. In which case, the salaries will follow."

They might respond: "You say 'higher' – how much higher?"

Hmm! Typical! Now, say you're on £25,000 at the moment and this new job requires management of more people, plus budget control and target cost reduction (both new). You now go for the highest figure you dare, without getting outrageous. The first time you try this, you will literally cringe inside as the words are caught in a vice-like grip in your guts. But remember, you will always be brought down. If you say you want at least 28k, they'll give you <u>at most</u> 28k. If you say £33,000, they may say £28,000 anyway. So be brave – you have nothing to lose.

The typical comment you get about salary is that there are already people there, with experience, who would pull a face if you were getting as much or more than them. What twaddle. People work side-by-side for years without knowing each other's salaries. How are they going to know unless they tell them? You're not going to tell them, right? In any case, you should be gauged on <u>your</u> abilities and potential, not theirs.

Another thing, be careful not to fall for the "you'll get a review in 6 months" trick, under the pretence that you need to 'prove yourself' first. Sure you'll get a review and then they will decide to give you half of nothing.

Instead, make sure it is stated in the contract that you'll get a 10% rise after 6 months – by that time you will have 'proved yourself' (i.e. you will still be there). By the way, if you think 10% is fair, ask for 15% or 20% at first. You'll get haggled back, of course, then when you finally settle for 10%, it will still seem like they're getting a good deal after all. *And* you can hold this concession against them at a later date.

An alternative is to distract their attention from your 20% with a 'red herring', such as a better car, which you didn't want in the first place. When they say you can't have one, you reluctantly concede the car on the condition that you get a better salary. If your increase is less than the extra cost of the car, you can make it look like you are doing them a favour, whereas you are in fact getting your own way. Masterful!

The trick is, when you do make a concession, ask for a trade off in return. Salaries compound every year. A little judicious work now could pay real dividends later on. So...study.

---

*(p.136) Generally, people are paid according to the responsibility they carry. A team-leader managing 20 people will not be paid as much as a project manager in charge of only 2 others, but who is devising a £10 million cap-ex project.

Closing Comment

That's it. You're done. Now it's time to put all of this into practice. There is a great deal of work to be gleaned from this book. If you want to get the most from it, you should go back and read it through again. This time, pause and make notes of points you need to learn more about and list the issues you need to work on, personally. It will be valuable preparation for your job hunting process.

Invest the time and effort now and you will put yourself in a commanding position in the modern job market for many years to come. Your own self-managed career path awaits you, detached from reliance on out-dated company training programmes and free from corporate rhetoric and the vagaries of the job market. Study the job market, analyse your own competencies and match the two. Work on your personal presentation and practice your answers. Read this book over again, so that your job-hunting strategy and interview technique become second nature. Apply yourself and the whole world of opportunity opens up before you.

I would wish you luck, but luck is for the unprepared, which doesn't include you. Instead, I will wish you every success. Bon voyage.

Appendix

Action Words For CVs

Below is a list of 1,000 'action' words that you can use on your CV as benefit-generators to boost the impact of the text of your CV. There is no need to scan them all; they can be cross-referenced in any Thesaurus, even the one on your PC. Simply look up or type in an approximate word and pick from the selection offered.

Abridged	Adjoined	Anticipated	Audited
Accelerated	Adjudged	Appealed	Augmented
Accentuated	Adjudicated	Appeased	Authenticated
Accepted	Adjusted	Appended	Authored
Acclaimed	Administered	Applied	Authorised
Accommodated	Adopted	Appointed	Automated
Accompanied	Advanced	Appraised	Averted
Accomplished	Advertised	Approached	Awarded
Accounted	Advised	Appropriated	Balanced
Accredited	Advocated	Approved	Banded
Accrued	Affected	Arbitrated	Beat
Accumulated	Affirmed	Arranged	Began
Achieved	Aided	Articulated	Beheld
Acknowledged	Aligned	Ascertained	Benefited
Acquired	Allocated	Assembled	Bestowed
Acted	Allotted	Asserted	Bid
Activated	Allowed	Assessed	Blended
Actuated	Altered	Assigned	Bolstered
Adapted	Amassed	Assimilated	Booked
Added	Amended	Assisted	Boosted
Addressed	Analysed	Attached	Bought
Adept	Animated	Attained	Briefed
Adhered	Announced	Attracted	Broached

139

Broadened	Commanded	Consulted	Deferred
Brought	Commenced	Contacted	Defined
Budgeted	Commissioned	Contained	Deflected
Built	Communicated	Contended	Delegated
Bundled	Compacted	Contested	Deliberated
Bypassed	Compared	Continued	Delighted
Calculated	Compelled	Contracted	Delineated
Calibrated	Competed	Contrasted	Delivered
Canvassed	Compiled	Contributed	Delved
Capable	Completed	Contrived	Demonstrated
Captured	Complied	Controlled	Denoted
Carved	Composed	Conversed	Depicted
Catalogued	Compounded	Converted	Described
Categorised	Compressed	Conveyed	Deserved
Caught	Comprised	Convinced	Designated
Caused	Computed	Cooperated	Designed
Celebrated	Computerised	Coordinated	Detailed
Centralised	Conceived	Corrected	Detected
Certified	Concentrated	Correlated	Determined
Chaired	Conceptualised	Corresponded	Developed
Challenged	Conciliated	Corroborated	Devised
Changed	Concluded	Counselled	Diagnosed
Characterised	Concurred	Counted	Dictated
Charged	Condensed	Countered	Differentiated
Charted	Conditioned	Crafted	Diminished
Chartered	Conducted	Created	Directed
Checked	Conferred	Critiqued	Disassembled
Chose	Configured	Cultivated	Discerned
Chronicled	Confirmed	Curbed	Discharged
Cited	Conformed	Curtailed	Disclosed
Clarified	Confronted	Customised	Disconnected
Classified	Congregated	Cut	Discontinued
Climbed	Connected	Dealt	Discovered
Closed	Conquered	Debated	Discussed
Coached	Conserved	Decided	Dislodged
Coalesced	Considered	Deciphered	Dismantled
Collaborated	Consigned	Decreased	Dismissed
Collated	Consolidated	Deduced	Dispatched
Collected	Constrained	Defeated	Dispensed
Combined	Constructed	Defended	Dispersed

Displaced	Enacted	Evaluated	Foresaw
Displayed	Encapsulated	Evened	Foretold
Disposed	Enclosed	Examined	Formed
Disproved	Encompassed	Exceeded	Formulated
Dissected	Encouraged	Excelled	Fortified
Disseminated	Endeavoured	Exchanged	Forwarded
Dissipated	Ended	Excited	Fostered
Distinguished	Endorsed	Executed	Found
Distributed	Endowed	Exercised	Founded
Diverged	Energised	Exerted	Fulfilled
Diverted	Enforced	Exhibited	Functioned as
Divided	Engaged	Expanded	Funded
Divulged	Engendered	Expedited	Furnished
Documented	Engineered	Expended	Furthered
Dominated	Enhanced	Experienced	Gained
Donated	Enjoyed	Experimented	Galvanized
Doubled	Enlarged	Expert	Gathered
Drafted	Enlightened	Explained	Gauged
Dramatised	Enlisted	Exposed	Gave
Drew	Enlivened	Expounded	Generated
Drilled	Enriched	Expressed	Gestured
Dropped	Enrolled	Expunged	Governed
Drove	Ensured	Extracted	Graded
Duplicated	Entailed	Extricated	Granted
Earned	Entered	Fabricated	Graphed
Edited	Entertained	Facilitated	Grasped
Educated	Enticed	Familiarised	Greeted
Effected	Enumerated	Fashioned	Grew
Elected	Enunciated	Featured	Grossed
Elevated	Epitomised	Filed	Grouped
Eliminated	Equalised	Filtered	Guaranteed
Elucidated	Equated	Finalised	Guarded
Embarked	Equipped	Financed	Guided
Embellished	Erected	Finished	Had
Embodied	Escalated	Fitted	Handled
Embraced	Escorted	Fixed	Harboured
Employed	Espoused	Followed	Harmonised
Empowered	Established	Followed up	Hastened
Emulated	Estimated	Forced	Heightened
Enabled	Evacuated	Forecasted	Held

Helped	Injected	Labelled	Merged
Highlighted	Innovated	Laboured	Merited
Hiked	Inquired	Launched	Meshed
Hindered	Inscribed	Learned	Met
Hired	Inserted	Lectured	Minimised
Honed	Inspected	Led	Ministered
Honoured	Inspired	Legalised	Mixed
Housed	Installed	Lessened	Mobilised
Hunted	Instigated	Levelled	Modelled
Hypothesised	Instituted	Liberated	Moderated
Idealised	Instructed	Licensed	Modernised
Identified	Instrumental	Lifted	Modified
Illuminated	Insulated	Limited	Moulded
Illustrated	Insured	Linked	Mollified
Imaged	Integrated	Listed	Monitored
Imagined	Intensified	Loaded	Motivated
Imitated	Interchanged	Lobbied	Mounted
Immersed	Interested	Located	Moved
Imparted	Interfaced	Looked	Multiplied
Implemented	Interjected	Lowered	Named
Implied	Interlaced	Made	Narrated
Impressed	Interpreted	Magnified	Navigated
Imprinted	Interrogated	Maintained	Negotiated
Improved	Intervened	Managed	Netted
Improvised	Interviewed	Manoeuvred	Neutralised
Inaugurated	Introduced	Manipulated	Nominated
Incited	Invalidated	Manufactured	Normalised
Included	Invented	Mapped	Noted
Incorporated	Invested	Marked	Noticed
Increased	Investigated	Marketed	Notified
Indexed	Invigorated	Massed	Nullified
Indicated	Involved	Mastered	Nurtured
Indoctrinated	Isolated	Masterminded	Observed
Induced	Issued	Matched	Obstructed
Inferred	Itemised	Maximised	Obtained
Inflated	Joined	Measured	Occupied
Influenced	Judged	Mediated	Offered
Informed	Justified	Mended	Officiated
Infused	Kept	Mentored	Offset
Initiated	Knowledgeable	Merchandised	Opened

Operated	Plotted	Proofed	Recaptured
Opposed	Pointed	Proofread	Received
Orchestrated	Policed	Propagandised	Reciprocated
Ordered	Polished	Propagated	Recited
Organised	Portrayed	Propelled	Reckoned
Originated	Positioned	Propitious	Recognised
Outdid	Possessed	Proposed	Recommended
Outfitted	Postponed	Protected	Reconciled
Outlined	Postulated	Proved	Reconditioned
Overcame	Practiced	Provided	Reconstructed
Overhauled	Predicted	Provoked	Recorded
Oversaw	Predominated	Pruned	Recounted
Packaged	Prepared	Publicised	Recovered
Packed	Prescribed	Published	Recreated
Paid	Presented	Purchased	Recruited
Painted	Preserved	Purged	Rectified
Paraphrased	Presided	Purified	Redeemed
Participated	Pressured	Pursued	Redesigned
Passed	Presumed	Pushed	Redirected
Patrolled	Prevailed	Qualified	Redoubled
Patterned	Prevented	Queried	Redrafted
Penetrated	Printed	Questioned	Reduced
Perceived	Prioritised	Quoted	Re-established
Perfected	Probed	Raised	Referred
Performed	Proceeded	Rallied	Refined
Permeated	Processed	Ran	Refreshed
Persuaded	Proclaimed	Ranked	Refuted
Petitioned	Procured	Rated	Regenerated
Photographed	Produced	Ratified	Registered
Phrased	Proficient	Rationalised	Regrouped
Picked	Profited	Reached	Regulated
Pictured	Programmed	Read	Rehabilitated
Pierced	Progressed	Readied	Rehearsed
Piloted	Prohibited	Realised	Reinforced
Pinpointed	Projected	Reaped	Reinstated
Pioneered	Prolonged	Rearranged	Reintroduced
Placed	Prominent	Reasoned	Reiterated
Planned	Promised	Reassembled	Related
Played	Promoted	Rebuilt	Relayed
Pledged	Pronounced	Recalled	Released

Relinquished	Retailored	Selected	Staffed
Relished	Retained	Sent	Staggered
Relocated	Retold	Separated	Standardised
Remade	Retrieved	Sequestered	Started
Remanded	Returned	Served	Stated
Remembered	Revamped	Serviced	Steadied
Remitted	Revealed	Set	Steered
Remodelled	Reversed	Set up	Stimulated
Removed	Reviewed	Settled	Stipulated
Rendered	Revised	Shadowed	Stirred
Renewed	Revitalised	Shaped	Stockpiled
Renovated	Revived	Sharpened	Stopped
Renowned	Revoked	Sheared	Stored
Reordered	Reworded	Sheltered	Stowed
Reorganised	Reworked	Shelved	Straightened
Repaired	Rewrote	Shielded	Streamlined
Repeated	Rose	Shifted	Strengthened
Replaced	Rotated	Shipped	Stressed
Replenished	Roused	Shortened	Stretched
Replied	Routed	Showed	Strived
Reported	Ruled	Sifted	Strove
Represented	Rushed	Signalled	Structured
Reproduced	Safeguarded	Signified	Studied
Reprogrammed	Salvaged	Simplified	Subjugated
Requested	Sanctioned	Sized	Submerged
Requisitioned	Satisfied	Sketched	Submitted
Rescued	Saved	Skilled	Substantiated
Researched	Scaled	Smoothed	Substituted
Reserved	Scanned	Snared	Succeeded
Reshaped	Scattered	Sold	Suggested
Resisted	Scheduled	Solicited	Summarised
Resolved	Scored	Solved	Superceded
Responded	Scouted	Soothed	Superintended
Restated	Screened	Sorted	Supervised
Restocked	Scrutinised	Sought	Supplanted
Restored	Searched	Sparked	Supplied
Restricted	Seasoned	Spearheaded	Supported
Restructured	Secured	Specified	Surmounted
Resulted in	Segregated	Spoke	Surpassed
Retailed	Seized	Stabilised	Surrendered

Surveyed	Totalled	Tutored	Varied
Sustained	Toughened	Twisted	Ventured
Switched	Toured	Typed	Verbalised
Symbolised	Traced	Uncoiled	Verified
Synchronised	Tracked	Uncovered	Versed
Synthesised	Traded	Underlined	Viewed
Systematised	Trained	Underscored	Vindicated
Tabulated	Transacted	Understood	Visited
Tackled	Transcribed	Undertook	Visualised
Tailored	Transferred	Underwrote	Vitalised
Talked	Transformed	Unearthed	Vocalised
Tallied	Translated	Unfolded	Voiced
Targeted	Transmitted	Unfurled	Volunteered
Taught	Transmuted	Unified	Warranted
Tempered	Transported	United	Watched
Tended	Transposed	Unmasked	Weaved
Tendered	Travelled	Unveiled	Weighed
Terminated	Treated	Updated	Welcomed
Tested	Tried	Upgraded	Widened
Theorised	Trimmed	Upheld	Witnessed
Tightened	Triumphed	Urged	Won
Timed	Troubleshot	Used	Worked
Titled	Truncated	Ushered	Wrapped
Took	Tuned	Utilised	Wrote
Took over	Turned	Validated	Yielded

Other Reading

"*What Colour Is Your Parachute*", Richard Nelson Bolles (Ten Speed Press).

"*Interviews, How To Succeed*", Judy Skeats (Templar Publishing, 1994).

"*Career Paths For The 21st Century*", Jim Durcan and David Oates, (Random House, 1996).

"*How To Build High Self-Esteem*", Jack Canfield (audio-cassette only from Nightingale-Conan Corporation, 1989).

"*The Psychology of Winning*", Dr. Denis Waitley (Berkley Publishing, 1995).

"*The Secrets Of Power Negotiating*", Roger Dawson (Career Press, 1999).

"*Assertiveness at Work*," Ken and Kate Back, (McGraw-Hill, 1999).

"*Understanding Organisations*", Charles Handy (Penguin, 1993).

"*The Practice of Management*", Peter F. Drucker (Butterworth-Heinemann, 1954).

"*Post Capitalist Society*", Peter F. Drucker (Butterworth-Heinemann, 1994).

ProFile Career Dynamics

Practical Strategies For Career Acceleration.

ProFile is a unique organisation designed to help you accelerate your career. ProFile's product range includes:

Courses – How to *Triple* your salary!
Studies show that those proficient in technicalities have an average salary of around £18,000. Those skilled in personal communication command around £55,000. These courses allow you to develop this lucrative skill.

CV Service
This book includes a step-by-step guide to producing your own killer CV. If you prefer to leave nothing to chance, ProFile will ensure your first impression is the strongest it can be.

Newsletter - "The Pro File"
The newsletter for the dedicated professional. Imagine if you had a personal coach sharing career-boosting secrets with you every week of the year... How successful would *you* become? Information, ideas, techniques, tips and advice to enhance your effectiveness, efficiency, professionalism and marketability. Quite simply, if you want to "make it", you have to know this stuff. Your first 6 issues are FREE.

FREE Careers Booklet and FREE Newsletter
See over the page for more details on these.

You can read more about each of these at the ProFile web site:

"www.career-dynamics.co.uk"

Your Career Is Your Livelihood
Protect It
Nurture It
Invest In It

FREE from ProFile Career Dynamics

**"10 Things They Never Tell You When You Start Work
...And Why!"**

The smart way to a more profitable career.
10 cutting insights into the world of work your boss would
rather you didn't know, including:

- ✓ 4 ways to slash your workload and *still* get more done.
- ✓ What bosses look for in promotional material.
- ✓ How to stand out as a prime promotional candidate.
- ✓ Why being popular can be bad for your career.
- ✓ Why your boss' anger is nothing to fear.
- ✓ The best way to make the most money from your job.

...so for goodness sake, don't show this to your boss!

Newsletter
Weekly e-mail bulletins from the world of work - advice,
insights and up-to-date info. from the jobs market. Available
on-line at: **www.career-dynamics.co.uk.**

—————————————

To obtain your Free booklet visit the ProFile web site at:
"www.career-dynamics.co.uk"

or write to:
FREEPOST NWW4718A, Manchester, M25 4BA

To your future prosperity.